LAW AND
MORALITY

LAW AND
MORALITY

Edited with an Introduction by
D. DON WELCH

FORTRESS PRESS   **Philadelphia**

Library of Congress Cataloging-in-Publication Data

Law and morality.

Bibliography: p.
Includes index.
1. Law—Philosophy. 2. Law and ethics. I. Welch, Don, 1947–
K235.L33 1987   340′.112   86-45195
ISBN 0-8006-1974-9

2565I86   Printed in the United States of America   1–1974

Contents

75709

Editor's Foreword

The debate about the relationship between law and morality has raged for centuries. At present, however, fresh insights into the nature of law are emerging as discussions of legal concepts are being launched from a variety of bases: critical legal studies, phenomenological hermeneutics, literary criticism, among others. At the same time, ethics as a field is expanding as new methods and issues become considered. This volume sets the stage for the renewed conversation that will inevitably follow the exploration of new perspectives on legal interpretation and morality.

The essays collected here have contributed significantly to our current understandings, presenting an overview of three major problems in law and morality and various approaches to them. Each piece represents an important perspective that must be considered in the current debate. The studies are much more than merely theoretical for they develop their theses directly in light of such contemporary moral and legal issues as racism, homosexuality, and genocide. I have introduced the entire discussion with an original essay that describes one way in which developing notions about the nature of law and morality can alter the grounds on which the subject is discussed.

Readers unfamiliar with these problems in law and morality will find that these essays provide a good starting point, while more advanced students can appreciate having these classical statements gathered together in one place. Operating within certain constraints, such as avoiding pieces that are too technical and observing limitations on length (which led to excerpting important essays whose inclusion was critical), I have attempted to include points of view from various disciplines on a problem that is truly too broad to be the captive of any academic specialty.

I wish to express my gratitude to the authors and their original publishers whose works are reprinted here. I am particularly indebted to Douglas Knight of Vanderbilt University and James Childress of the University of Virginia for their wisdom and advice in the shaping of this project.

D. DON WELCH
Vanderbilt University

Acknowledgments

Lord Patrick Devlin, "Morals and the Criminal Law," is reprinted from *The Enforcement of Morals* (New York and London: Oxford University Press, 1965) 1–25 by permission of Oxford University Press. Copyright © 1965 by Oxford University Press.

H. L. A. Hart, "Law, Liberty, and Morality," is excerpted by permission from *Law, Liberty, and Morality* (Stanford, Calif.: Stanford University Press, 1963). Copyright © 1963 by Stanford University Press.

Frederick S. Carney, "Religion and the Legislation of Morals," is reprinted by permission from *Soundings* 51 (1968) 432–47. Copyright © by *Soundings*.

H. L. A. Hart, "Positivism and the Separation of Law and Morals," is excerpted by permission from *Harvard Law Review* 71 (1958) 593–629. Copyright © 1958 by the Harvard Law Review Association.

Lon L. Fuller, "Positivism and Fidelity to Law—A Reply to Professor Hart," is excerpted by permission from *Harvard Law Review* 71 (1958) 630–72. Copyright © 1958 by the Harvard Law Review Association.

Douglas Sturm, "Three Contexts of Law," is reprinted from *Journal of Religion* 47 (1964) 127–45 by permission of the author and the University of Chicago Press. Copyright © 1964 by the University of Chicago Press.

Michael Walzer, "The Obligation to Disobey the Law," is reprinted from *Obligations: Essays on Disobedience, War, and Citizenship* (Cambridge, Mass.: Harvard University Press, 1970) 3–23 by permission of the author. The article appeared previously in *Political Theory and Social Change* (ed. David Spitz; Chicago: Atherton Press,

1967) 187–202, and *Ethics* 77 (1967) 163–75. Copyright © 1967 by Atherton Press.

Martin Luther King, Jr., "Letter from Birmingham City Jail," is reprinted from *Why We Can't Wait* (New York: Harper & Row, 1963) 152–68 by permission of Harper & Row, Publishers, Inc. Copyright © 1963 by Martin Luther King, Jr.

Emil Brunner and Karl Barth, "A Correspondence," is reprinted by permission from *Against the Stream* by Karl Barth, translated by E. M. Delacour and Stanley Godman; edited by Ronald Gregor Smith (New York: Philosophical Library; London: SCM Press, 1954) 106–18. Copyright © 1954 by SCM Press and Philosophical Library, Inc.

The Contributors

LORD PATRICK DEVLIN was a judge of the Queen's Bench from 1948 to 1960 and was created a Lord of Appeal in 1961. His most famous lectures on law and morality are collected in *The Enforcement of Morals.*

H. L. A. HART was formerly Professor of Jurisprudence in the University of Oxford. His landmark publications include *The Concept of Law; Law, Liberty, and Morality*; and *Punishment and Responsibility.*

FREDERICK S. CARNEY is Professor of Ethics at Perkins School of Theology, Southern Methodist University, and has published widely in the area of contemporary moral and legal philosophy.

LON L. FULLER was Carter Professor of Jurisprudence at Harvard University. His publications include *The Morality of Law* and *Legal Fictions.*

DOUGLAS STURM is Professor of Religion and Political Science at Bucknell University. He has published several articles on social and legal philosophy in both religious and legal journals.

MICHAEL WALZER is Professor in the School of Social Science at the Institute of Advanced Study. He has written *Obligations: Essays on Disobedience, War, and Citizenship; Spheres of Justice: A Defense of Pluralism and Equality*; and *Radical Principles: Reflections of an Unreconstructed Democrat.*

MARTIN LUTHER KING, JR., theologian and civil rights leader, was awarded the Nobel Prize for Peace in 1964. Among his published works are *Stride Toward Freedom* and *Why We Can't Wait.*

EMIL BRUNNER was Chair of Systematic and Practical Theology at the University of Zurich, while often visiting as a lecturer at leading centers of theological education in the United States and Europe. His numerous publications include *The Divine Imperative.*

KARL BARTH, noted Swiss theologian, held chairs of theology at Basel, Göttingen, Münster, and Bonn. His many books include *Community, State, and Church* and *Church Dogmatics.*

Introduction:
The Moral Dimension of Law

D. Don Welch

An experience common to all persons is answering the question, What ought I to do? This normative question, demanding choice and action, is a fundamental part of our lives. When we examine the way we answer that question, we discover that our choices and actions have their source in moralities that we have chosen and that have chosen us—in norms, values, goals, dispositions, and intentions that shape our response to the world around us.

These moralities are a product of faith, of one's vision of what is ultimately good or worthy of loyalty. While "faith" often has religious connotations, this kind of affirmation of ultimate value can be religious, nonreligious, or even antireligious. Sometimes this faith has been intentionally developed and nurtured; sometimes it is a mass of unexamined assumptions. In each case, this faith reflects the allegiance we give to fundamental realities as sources of value and as objects of loyalty. Out of this faith we fashion a stance toward life, a prism through which we interpret reality. This faith is the foundation for the morality that determines, although not in a mechanical way, our response to the question, What ought I to do?

As citizens of modern nation-states, we live under another "ought." We are subject to legal rules, to laws that proscribe some behaviors and mandate others. These laws do not simply mediate the preferences and choices of our community, or some segment of that community. These laws are part of a reward and punishment system that aims to coerce, when necessary, behavior that conforms to a view of the kind of society we should have. The question of whether a law ought to exist is separate from the fact that the existence of that law must be taken into account when a citizen decides what he or she should do.

The law and morals problem is easily described. When choosing what we ought to do, we are responding to two "oughts" (among others): one grounded in this basic faith, the other encountered in the law. Since these two sources of norms are, to a degree, independent sources for any individual, there exists the possibility of discrepancies between the choices they endorse. As persons of faith and as persons living under the law, we must decide how to distinguish between, and how to relate, the moralities of faith and the dictates of law. This task is not an abstract academic exercise. The decisions we make on this issue, whether made intentionally or by default, set the boundaries for our response to that basic question, What ought I to do?

The problem of the relationship between law and morality is present in all cultures and societies—although the examples in this volume are limited to the common law traditions of the United States and the United Kingdom. Moreover, the interaction between law and morals is not simply a problem for "personal" ethics. Profound public policy implications flow from the way a community characterizes the relationship between these two areas of life. Different societies have chosen different paths, ranging from the domination of the legal structure by the religious establishment in a theocracy to the attempts in some modern nation-states to divorce completely the affairs of state from any appeal to religious warrants.

The essays included in this volume are important twentieth-century contributions to the discussion of three aspects of the law-and-morality problem: the legal enforcement of morality, the interrelation of law and morality, and moral objections to law. This introduction serves a dual purpose: to introduce these essays and the issues they raise, and to provide a critique of the way in which the nature of morality and, by extension, the nature of law have been presented in major writings in this field. An understanding of law and morals, based on relational value theory, is offered as a way of clarifying some central issues and moving consideration of the subject into more productive avenues.

The Interrelation of Law and Morality

Scholarly examination of this relationship has produced treatises and essays which explore each nuance of sophisticated arguments and complex theories. At the same time, every person has had to come to terms with law and morality in everyday life. Each of us recognizes and responds to legal and moral obligations. Each of us—however unreflectively—has fashioned a personal stance that guides our thoughts and actions as we respond to the expectations we encounter in law and morality and in the interaction between them.

Some interaction between law and morality appears to be beyond dispute. Morality serves as a source in the development of law, and law serves as a source in the development of morality. Law develops as an expression of a societal morality. The law reflects the values a community chooses to enhance, the rights it chooses to protect, and the goals it chooses to pursue. Citizens, legislators, administrative officials, judges, and jurors create law, and their own perceptions of what is just, right, fair, and true influence them. H. L. A. Hart writes of the manifold ways in which morality has determined the course of law, "sometimes covertly and slowly through the judicial process, sometimes openly and abruptly through legislation,"[1] and—I would add—most starkly through civil disobedience and revolution.

On the other hand, law serves as a source for morality. The old cliché, You can't legislate morality, simply is not true. If morality refers to the way people behave, the law obviously shapes morality. When citizens are making decisions about what they ought to do, the legal "ought" usually plays a major role in the decision process. In a more fundamental way the law is a source for morality when morality is viewed as beliefs and values that guide our choices. The perception of what is legal or illegal affects one's perception of what is moral or immoral. The weight of that community judgment is felt throughout the citizenry. Legally mandated changes in social structures create circumstances and experiences that alter moral attitudes as one gains new information, discards old prejudices, finds new "authorities," shares new group perceptions, responds to new societal pressures, and develops new views of reality.

In a similar vein, just as law is a source for morality and morality a source for law, so the operation of the law has moral implications and the application of moral norms has legal implications. As the law shapes and alters our lives and actions, some moral values are enhanced and some are demeaned. Certain moral purposes are furthered and others frustrated by the reward and punishment system established by law. Morality has legal implications when, for example, we refer to community moral standards to give content to a host of legal notions such as due process, equal protection, the right to privacy, cruel and unusual punishment, obscenity, and in the jury process of sentencing and even determining guilt and innocence. Laws lose their force when they lose popular backing, and the meaning of legal rules changes as a society changes its views of the kind of legal order it wants.

While the intertwining of law and morality suggested in this widely accepted proposition is extensive, the two realities are not coextensive. Legal obligation is distinct from moral obligation. Some aspects of our lives seem appropriate for moral regulation but not legal control. Legal norms are subject to criticism from a moral point of view, and a plurality of moralities within a given community must be limited by and subject to a common legal order. It is this "separateness" of law and morality that moves us beyond these initial observations, which address propositions which command general acceptance, and that gives rise to the three questions which command the primary attention in this essay.

The first of these questions, as asked by Lord Patrick Devlin in the first article reprinted in this volume, is: "What is the connection between crime and sin and to what extent, if at all, should the criminal law . . . concern itself with the enforcement of morals and punish sin or immorality as such?"[2] The issue has been labeled "The Legal Enforcement of Morality" and is the subject of the renowned exchange between Devlin and Hart.[3] While the exchange between these scholars was prompted by the possible decriminalization of homosexual behavior between consenting adults in private, their arguments can be applied to all efforts to regulate human behavior by law.

In a very important sense this is a simple question, and much of the discussion of the issue has missed the point. Should morality be enforced by law? Of course it should. What other grounds exist for outlawing certain behavior? What do we enforce through law if it is not some person's or some group's perception of morality?

All legal theories justify certain kinds of enforcement of morals in . the sense that they support laws which have their source in morality and which have moral implications. All laws reflect the choice of one value or set of values over others. The antithesis to Lord Devlin's affirmation of the enforcement of morals is the position taken by John Stuart Mill. His often-quoted statement from *On Liberty* is: "[T]he only purpose for which power can be rightfully exercised over any member of a civilized community, against his will, is to prevent harm to others."[4] Hart calls this an "emphatic negative answer" to the question of whether morality should be enforced by law. In fact, however, Mill's comment is a statement about which morality he believes should be enforced by law, and which should not.

This clarification brings us to the crux of the legal enforcement of morals issue. The question is not whether morality should be legally enforced, but rather which morality should be supported in this way. Making and interpreting laws inevitably involves moral choices. The issue is whether there is a limit to the way in which morality should be turned into law and, if so, to determine how that limit should become part of the legal process. This, in itself, is a moral question. Therefore, an appropriate answer can be given only in the context of a particular moral system.

An answer to the question of the appropriate limits on the legal enforcement of morality is best understood after another question is addressed: Can an adequate definition of law be established apart from considerations of morality? This issue is the subject of the Hart-Fuller debate, captured in the first two essays in the second section of reprinted articles.[5] Again, the impact of these articles ranges beyond the particular example on which they focused, the extent to which the statutes and judicial decisions of the Third Reich are to be considered laws.

As background for understanding the exchange between Hart and Lon L. Fuller, it is important to keep in mind the centuries-old natural law tradition which held, in essence, that an immoral law is not really a law. In the thirteenth century Saint Thomas Aquinas provided one of the most enduring expressions of this point of view:

> Human law has the nature of law in so far as it partakes of right reason; and it is clear that, in this respect, it is derived from eternal law. But in so far as it deviates from reason, it is called an unjust law, and has the nature, not of law, but of violence.[6]

The same sentiment was expressed by the most prominent jurist of eighteenth-century English law, Sir William Blackstone.

> [The] law of nature, being coeval with mankind and dictated by God himself, is of course superior in obligation to any other. It is binding over all the globe in all countries, and at all times; no human laws are of any validity, if contrary to this: and such of them as are valid derive all their force, and all their authority, mediately or immediately, from this original.[7]

More recently, Martin Luther King, Jr., aligned himself with this view of the necessity of morality in legality as he wrote in his *Letter from Birmingham City Jail,* "I would agree with Saint Augustine that 'An unjust law is no law at all.'"[8]

As a challenge to this requirement of a moral test for determining the validity of law, two English utilitarians developed an approach to law that came to be labeled legal positivism. Jeremy Bentham and John Austin sought to establish clearly the important distinction between law as it actually exists and law as it ought to be. Austin, for example, wrote: "[T]he existence of law is one thing; its merit or demerit is another. Whether it be or be not is one enquiry; whether it be or be not conformable to an assumed standard, is a different enquiry."[9]

Bentham and Austin wanted to establish that a rule did not cease to be a rule of law simply because it violated a moral standard, and, conversely, that the fact that a rule was law did not answer the moral question. As Hart has summarized, "They were concerned to argue that such laws, even if morally outrageous, were still laws."[10] In the words of Hans Kelsen, "Legal norms may have any kind of content. . . . The validity of a legal norm cannot be questioned on the ground that its contents are incompatible with some moral or political value."[11] A summary statement of the legal positivist perspective on the relation between law and morality has been offered by David A. J. Richards: "Laws are not, as a matter of definition or fact, always or necessarily moral."[12] In order to discern the significance of this statement, and then to evaluate its adequacy, it is helpful to think of the meaning of "moral" in two different senses—as a descriptive term and as a judgmental or normative term.

In the descriptive sense, "moral" is opposed to "nonmoral," meaning that a group or person's morals or morality consists of whatever attitudes or beliefs the group or person holds about the propriety of human conduct, values, or goals. "Moral" in this sense is not used approvingly, but simply to indicate the nature of the subject (i.e., related to values) being discussed. If "moral" is understood in this sense, Richards's statement is clearly false. Laws do address matters of human conduct, values, and goals. Indeed, a subsequent statement by Richards indicates that he was not using "moral" in this descriptive sense: "Laws and legal systems are instruments of moral purposes and ideals; as such, they are embedded in a context of moral principles which often alone explain the form of legal doctrine."[13]

In the judgmental sense "moral" is the opposite of "immoral." We speak of acts or views being moral, meaning we judge them to be good, right, or appropriate. In these terms, the positivist proposition is that laws are not necessarily right or good.

The moral pluralism of the contemporary world poses problems for the positivist position. To say that a law is a law even if it is not moral is a puzzling statement when we realize that the law would not be a law in the first place if it did not conform to some view of morality. And, given the competing moralities in our society, virtually all laws will be judged and found wanting from one moral perspective or another.

Another way of construing Richards's summary of the positivist position is to interpret "moral" to refer to the general, consensual morality of a particular community. Construed in this way, the statement would assert that laws do not necessarily conform to the basic values of the society which enacts them. There are several problems with this interpretation. First, this construction of the statement is not responsive to the arguments to which the positivists were reacting. Second, there is not a fixed, uncontested account of what a society's basic values are. Third, if we attempt to measure the fit between a law and societal morality by the general acceptance of a law within the community, the statement may violate other positivist views of the nature of law.

Is it plausible to interpret Richards's statement to mean that laws do not necessarily conform to a society's morality, as indicated by a lack of acceptance of them? This proposition would hold that laws are laws if duly enacted, even if they are widely disregarded or resisted. In his seminal *The Concept of Law,* Hart establishes as a necessary condition for the existence of a legal system that the laws which are valid (according to the system's criteria for validity) must be generally obeyed.[14] It may be that this criteria of obedience applies only in a generalized sense, that general obedience to "most" laws validates a legal "system," and that this standard does not apply in judging particular laws. But this distinction between "law" and legal system is not made in Hart's phrasing of the question underlying the Hart-Fuller debate: "Must some reference to morality enter into an adequate definition of law or legal system?"[15] Since Hart proposes a negative answer to this question and since he includes general obedience as a necessary condition for a valid legal system, it appears that Hart means something by "moral" other than societal acceptance.

The major problem, however, with this last interpretation of the summary statement—that laws do not have to conform to a society's morality—is that it is one with which the positivists' opponents would agree. When Augustine, Aquinas, Blackstone, and Martin

Luther King, Jr., among others, declare that unjust laws are not really laws, their reference is to some external normative standard, not to a certain prevailing moral environment at a particular time and place. Indeed, for a natural law proponent the danger in legal positivism is precisely the fear that the validity of law *is* related to a specific community rather than to objective moral principles. Thus, this rendition of the Richards's quotation states the position he is arguing against.

This brings us to a final alternative for understanding Richards's statement, one that makes sense of the positivist response to natural law theories and reveals the basic flaw in the positivists' position. When a legal philosopher says, "Laws are not, as a matter of definition or fact, always or necessarily moral," he or she is affirming the positivist proposition that a legal obligation and a moral obligation may not be identical, and that those conflicting obligations can be recognized without denying the validity of either. This principle seems to be well embedded in twentieth-century consciousness.[16] In winning this argument, however, the positivists have allowed the natural law theorists to dictate that the argument be waged on the wrong grounds. The only way this formulation makes sense is to accept the natural law assumption that there does exist an objective moral standard to which the law can be compared. The positivist does not believe that standard to be relevant for ascertaining the validity of a law, but the nature of the response indicates an acceptance of that assumption about the nature of morality. Implicit in the kind of statement Richards makes is the view that theoretically there is an objective morality by which laws could be judged moral or immoral. It is irrelevant whether or not one believes such judgments are pertinent to legality or even whether one believes that such judgments cannot, with certainty, be made. The acceptance of that first principle—that such an objective morality does exist—misconstrues the nature of morality, the nature of law, and the relationship between them.

Responsibility and Relational
Value Theory

An alternative conception of morality is worthy of attention at this point. The conception of morality developed in the model of responsibility presented by H. Richard Niebuhr in *The Responsible Self*[17] allows us to recast the traditional arguments in a helpful manner.

Niebuhr proposes the symbol of the person-as-answerer as an image which helps us understand the way moral decisions ("moral" in this context is being used in the descriptive sense discussed above) are made. This image of the person-as-answerer is presented by Niebuhr in contrast to two classical images that have dominated moral philosophy: the person-as-maker (teleological theory) and the person-as-citizen (deontological theory). According to teleological theory, the ultimate criterion of what is morally right, wrong, or obligatory is the value of what is brought into being as a consequence of the act being judged. The final appeal, directly or indirectly, must be to the good produced, or to the comparative balance of good over evil produced. The most common teleological approach is utilitarianism, which holds that an act is right if and only if it produces or is intended to produce at least as great a balance of good over evil in the universe as any available alternative.

Teleologists take different views about the ultimate good by which acts are to be judged. Some teleologists have been hedonists, identifying good with pleasure and evil with pain. Others have identified good with power, knowledge, self-realization, perfection, and so forth. They hold in common a basic symbol of the human person as a maker, a fashioner. What are human beings like in their actions? They are like artisans who construct things according to ideas and for the sake of ends. It is this end, this product or result, by which an act is judged to be good or bad, right or wrong.

Each of us knows what it is to act with a purpose, with a future state of affairs in mind. Everyone knows also how important it is to evaluate the steps taken moment by moment in this movement toward the desired goal. Many moral theories and moral exhortations presuppose the future-directed, purposive character of human action and differ among themselves only in the ends that are recommended or that are accepted as given with human nature itself. Each of these conforms to an image of the person-as-maker, the person viewed as technician or artisan.

The second grand image of the general character of our lives as moral agents is the image of the person-as-citizen living under the law, a deontological approach. Deontological theories assert that there are considerations which make an action or rule right or obligatory other than the goodness or badness or its consequences—that is, certain features of the act itself other than the value it brings into existence. A deontologist contends that it is possible for an action or rule of action to be the morally right or obligatory one even if it does not promote the greatest possible balance of good over evil. An act, for example, may be good because it keeps a promise, is just, or is commanded by God.

The moral philosophers and theologians who view persons primarily as citizens point out a deficiency in the person-as-maker model. Unlike the artisan, we control neither the material with which we work (ourselves, our neighbors, our historical circumstances) nor the products of our future building. Our lives, these moralists argue, are more like politics than art, and politics is the art of the possible. We come to self-awareness in the midst of mores, of commandments and rules, thou shalts and thou shalt nots, of directions and permissions. We must take account of the rule of the mores, of the ethos, of approvals and disapprovals, of social, legal, and religious sanctions.

Thus, the moral question is not what end shall I pursue, but what rule should I follow; not what shall I strive for, but what should I obey. We come into being under the rules of family, neighborhood, and nation, subject to the regulation of our action by others. Against these rules we can and do rebel, yet we find it necessary—morally necessary—to consent to some laws and to give ourselves rules, to administer our lives in accordance with some discipline.

Those who consistently think of the person-as-maker subordinate the giving of laws to construction. For them the right is to be defined by reference to the good; rules are utilitarian in character. They are the means to ends. All laws must justify themselves by the contribution they make to the attainment of a desired end. Those, however, who think of our existence primarily with the aid of the citizen image likewise seek to subordinate the good to the right; only right life is good, and right life is no future ideal but always a present demand.

In Niebuhr's alternative approach to the moral life, the symbolism of responsibility is important. Implicit in this idea of responsibility is the image of the person-as-answerer, the person engaged in dialogue, acting in response to action upon her or him. We have all experienced engagement in dialogue, answering questions addressed to us, defending ourselves against attacks, replying to injunctions, and meeting challenges. Following from these experiences, it may be helpful to think of all our actions as having this character of being responsive, answers to actions upon us. Biology, sociology, psychology, and other disciplines have taught us to regard ourselves as being in the midst of a field of natural and social forces, acted upon and reacting. Understanding ourselves as responsive beings is illuminating for considering moral questions. This understanding leads to an approach to our conduct that begins with neither purposes nor laws, but with responses.

In something of a summary statement, we may say that the

teleologist seeks to answer that question, What shall I do? by first asking: What is my goal, my ideal, or my teleos? Deontology tries to answer the moral query by asking, first of all: What is the law, and what is the fundamental law of my life? Responsibility, however, proceeds in every moment of decision and choice to inquire, What is going on? If we use value terms, then the differences among the three approaches may be indicated by the terms the good, the right, and the fitting. Teleology is concerned always with the highest good to which it subordinates the right; consistent deontology is concerned with the right no matter what may happen to our goods; but for the ethics of responsibility the *fitting* action, the one that fits into a total interaction as response and as anticipation of further response, is alone conducive to the good and alone is right.

Niebuhr identifies particular elements in the moral decision-making process within the responsibility model.[18] All our moral actions are responses to interpreted action upon us. We respond as we interpret the meaning of the world we encounter, and as we anticipate responses to our responses. We decide and act in a continuing discourse or interaction among persons that comprise a continuing society.

Thus, when we follow Niebuhr's scheme, we conceive of decisions which answer the question, What ought I to do? not as decisions which select a particular goal and the means to reach that goal, nor as decisions which sort through particular laws we have encountered and select which law should be followed. Rather, we think of this question as asking how we should respond to actions upon us, as we interpret those actions and as we anticipate response from other persons to our decisions and actions.

A vital part of this responsibility model for morality is the theory of value which gave rise to it—a value theory that is quite different from that implied by the arguments about law we considered in the preceding section. Important distinctions can be made between three different types of theories of value: objective theories, subjective theories, and relational theories. Objective value theory operates on the premise that there are certain values, certain definitions of good or right, that exist as objective facts in the universe. This approach to morality assumes that our task is to discover what is right or good and then apply it to our lives. The act required is one of discovery, because standards for conduct already exist, whether they are rooted in natural rights, or divine law, or the logical structures of human consciousness.

A second value theory is subjective theory. The proponents of this view tend to discount the validity of obligations incurred from values because such values are seen as relative to particular societies or even to particular individuals. A relativist often dismisses the terms "value" and "good" as nothing but expressions of an emotion. Relativism is fed by comparative cultural studies, which have led some people to conclude that since what is right differs radically from one society to another, right has no power at all: value is viewed as simply the summary of what a particular group of persons has decided to use to order its life.

The third approach is relational value theory, which is objective in the sense that value relations are understood to be independent of the feelings of an observer, but not in the sense that value is itself an objective kind of reality. Relational theory, as it is developed by Niebuhr in his seminal essay "The Center of Value,"[19] agrees with objectivism in that what is good for a person, or for a society, is not determined simply by the desire of that person or persons. Yet, relational value theory does not pretend that value has existence in itself, that independence from desire is equivalent to independence from the being for which the value has worth. The fundamental premise of relational value theory is that value is present as persons confront persons. Good is a term which should be applied to those realities which meet the needs, which fit the capacities, which correspond to the potentialities of persons.

Thus, it makes sense to talk about what is right or wrong only in relation to the individuals asking the question. Relational value theory understands that being and value are inseparably connected but that value cannot be identified with a certain mode of being or with any being considered in isolation. If anything existed simply in itself and by itself, value would not be present. Value is the good-for-ness of being for being in their interaction and their mutual aid. Value cannot be defined or intuited in itself, for it has no existence in itself. Nothing is valuable in itself, but everything has value, positive or negative, in its relations. Thus, value is not a relation but arises in the relations of being to being.

A relational understanding of law is emerging as recent developments in other disciplines are brought to bear on legal theory. Notable examples with some affinity for the approach taken in this essay include the work of Stanley Fish in applying principles of literary criticism to legal interpretation (see "Working on the Chain Gang: Interpretation in Law and Literature," *Critical Inquiry* 9 [1982]

201–216; and "Fish v. Fiss," *Stanford Law Review* 36 [1984] 1325–1347) and the use of phenomenological hermeneutics by Teresa Godwin Phelps and Jenny Ann Pitts ("Questioning the Text: The Significance of Phenomenological Hermeneutics for Legal Interpretation," *St. Louis University Law Journal* 29 [1985] 353–382).

Richard H. Hiers has made "a few concluding suggestions" about the relevance of relational value theory for law, drawing directly from H. Richard Niebuhr ("Normative Analysis in Judicial Determination of Public Policy," *The Journal of Law and Religion* 3 [1985] 77–115), and Gidon Gottlieb has identified the features of a "Relational Juridical System" ("Relationism: Legal Theory for a Relational Society," *University of Chicago Law Review* 50 [1983] 567–612). Missing in the discussion, however, is an assessment of the importance of relational theory for the particular issues of law and morality. This essay is a first step in that direction.

Relational Theory and the Law

Morality is not relegated to some compartment of our lives in which we make certain types of decisions based upon things we call moral rules or moral ends. Rather, morality encompasses the way we respond to all of life as we continually answer the question, What ought I to do? The law is one facet of our lives that impinges on this question of "ought." In this sense, legal questions are a subset of the larger moral question. Our decisions involving the law are not matters of determining a moral obligation and a legal obligation and then choosing between the two. Our decisions are responses to a variety of factors that impinge upon us—religious principles, financial calculations, legal statutes, professional standards, interpersonal commitments, social goals, psychic stress—as we seek to interpret our life situation and determine what action is most appropriate in that context.

The importance of emphasizing this sense of legal obligation as a subset of the moral question is the reminder that we should not allow people to deceive themselves into thinking they have avoided the moral question by restricting their reasoning to the legal question. It is never enough to justify one's actions by resorting, as a final argument, to the statement that "I was only obeying the law." When such an answer is given, the inquiry can be pushed: Why was your perception of what the law required determinative for your decision? It is a rare person who believes that the judgment of the state is the ultimate ground for morality. As a practical matter, individuals may "automatically" obey the law. But reflection upon such decisions makes clear that we fulfill a perceived legal obligation because we see that act as fitting into a larger pattern of what we deem to be good.

Answering the question, Is it moral? does not determine the answer to the question, Is it legal? But to state that I am doing X because it is required by law, even though I think it is wrong, is confusing. This type of statement seems to express the contradictory position, "I've decided I ought to obey the law and thus ought to do X, but I don't think I ought to do X." Rather than portraying such a case as choosing one "ought" over a conflicting "ought," we should see this as a case in which a legal "ought" is a part of the relational context which shapes our decisions about what we ought to do. What is really being said is, "*If* it weren't for this law, I should not do X." That law, however, does exist, just as in other circumstances promises, family ties, social contracts, and other realities exist which constitute the context for decision making.

The nature of law makes a perceived legal obligation a very powerful ingredient in the mix that we consider as we decide upon a responsible course of action. There are a number of reasons why a law carries such weight in our deliberations: a belief that the kind of world we want depends upon the social order created by general obedience to law; a sense of obligation owed in return for benefit received from the existing legal structure; an awareness of the pain and loss that may well be consequences of breaking a law. These kinds of reasons create a prima facie case for obeying the law. We thus often find that our perception of what the law requires in a particular situation provides the answer to the question: What ought I to do? Even these reasons, however, are moral reasons. This kind of legal obligation depends upon our moral judgment about the kind of society we want or the kind of pain and loss we are unwilling to endure.

The law has force for us in the way we respond to our world as it fits within our scheme of ultimate loyalties. In his essay reproduced in this book, Douglas Sturm speaks of "an object that is of final importance for human existence—an object of devotion, a matter of ultimate concern, a reality that constitutes the source of value and object of loyalty."[20] It is this basic faith, our commitment to certain causes and realities, which serves as a warrant for whatever authority law has for us. Law does not stand over against us, deserving of fidelity on its own account. It is only a piece of the grander interactive process which yields our choices of appropriate response. Our faiths may be grounded in different realities: a reverence for human life, a commitment to act only on universalizable principles, the greatest good for the greatest number. For Niebuhr, the ground of his faith was a radically monotheistic God as revealed in the Judeo-Christian tradition.

Sturm identifies this broader framework within which we view law as the "religious-humanistic context," in contrast to the "strictly legal context" of Hart's work and Fuller's "social context."[21] This broader faith perspective not only informs our choice of responses to the world we encounter (including the law), but even provides the interpretive lens through which we give meaning to the world to which we are responding.

This insight brings us back to the significance of relational value theory for law and morality. The model implied by the Hart and Fuller readings discussed earlier seems to run something like the following: (1) There exists something objective called Morals; (2) and something objective called Law. (3) The decision-maker sits back and observes these at a distance. (4) When there appears to be some dispute between Morals and Law, the observer makes some decision which (5) could be determined to be the right or wrong decision from some ideal point of view.

The problem with this model is that the very meaning of the law, in addition to its authority, is dependent upon values and interpretation (this is true, of course, for morality as well). Our perception of the law as an objective reality with a fixed meaning is due to the large areas of consensus that exist among us. Our shared values and meaning structures can become so taken for granted that we lose sight of this aspect of legal reasoning. Our value preferences lead us to choose one possible meaning of a statute over another plausible meaning, and to color and shade the meanings of particular words in a judicial precedent to fit our sense of what is appropriate in a given situation. When faced with language that does not admit to an appropriate interpretation, we speak of the spirit rather than the letter of the law, and judges denounce formalistic applications of the plain meaning of a statute because they lead to absurd consequences[22] or defeat the purpose of the law. In these types of cases, we are forced to recognize that we give meaning to law out of a matrix of beliefs and value preferences. The process in routine cases is not different from that in "hard cases." It only appears so because a consensus on beliefs and values produces what seems to be an automatic decision.

A movement is growing in legal academic circles which takes up this theme. Roberto Mangabeira Unger, one of the leading advocates of the Critical Legal Studies Movement, has described the "formalism" which he opposes as "commitment to, and therefore also a belief in the possibility of, a method of legal justification that can be clearly contrasted to open-ended disputes about the basic terms of social life, disputes that people call ideological, philosophical, or visionary."[23] From a very different jurisprudential camp, Harold Berman writes: "Law is not only a body of rules; it is people legislating, adjudicating, administering, negotiating—it is a living process of allocating rights and duties and thereby resolving conflicts and creating channels of cooperation."[24]

Thus, the discussion of a separation of law and morals is misplaced. We do not make decisions about the force of law—indeed, we do not make decisions about the meaning of law—apart from our morality. There is no value-free interpretation of law. Law does not exist as a thing in itself, apart from the significance given to it in a specific social context.

Niebuhr's model of moral action provides an image that also applies to the way law has meaning in our lives. The process of responding to interpreted action in anticipation of the response of others describes activity in the legal arena—as it does in other areas of moral concern. The judge on the bench interprets the facts and statements of law in a given case, responding to those in anticipation of responses from appellate judges, other members of the judicial panel, legal commentators, legislators, lawyers, and citizens contemplating activity in the given area in the future.[25] The same is true of legislators, lawyers, and private citizens. In each case, the law is understood and is given meaning as an actor responds to words and situations, anticipating the response that he or she will encounter from the legal and broader social community.

Consider the statute that is "on the books" which has fallen into disuse, widely ignored and even unknown to citizens and those in control of the law enforcement machinery. No one responds as if it were law. What sense does it make to talk as if this were a law? A collection of words has the force of law when it is interpreted as law, when people respond to it in anticipation that others will treat those linguistic symbols as law. A statement's significance as law is dependent upon this process of response and interpretation. As Stanley Fish has argued, laws do not have meaning before they are encountered in specific situations; they do not stand outside a field of practice that they can guide or control in appropriate ways. In his words, "[R]ules, in law or anywhere else, do not stand in an independent relationship to a field of action on which they can simply be imposed; rather, rules have a circular or mutually interdependent relationship to the field of action in that they make sense only in reference to the very regularities they are thought to bring about."[26]

This discussion cannot ignore what Hart identifies as the positivist's concern that we should keep separate "law as it is" and "law as it ought to be." We have all had the experience of encountering legal sanctions or edicts which contradict our own sense of what the law ought to be. It is more useful, however, to think of these as conflicts between differing concepts of what the law ought to be, rather than between law as it is and law as it ought to be. First, these conflicts often involve varying interpretations of what a statute means or of how a precedent applies in a particular set of circumstances. Second, even when the conflict exists because an observer thinks that the legislature or court made a mistake, it is helpful to construe this as a conflict of "oughts." The law would not "exist" if some person or body of persons did not think that it ought to exist. We are not in danger, in these types of cases, of forgetting that the words in a law do exist. There is a tendency, however, among persons who think the law ought to be different than it is, to forget that any moral judgment on a law is a relational judgment. The moral standard being used to criticize the existence of a given law is not an objective absolute, but grows out of a particular faith stance. Characterizing the conflict as one of competing views of what the law ought to be keeps this relational perspective in focus and moves us beyond the Hart-Fuller discussion of the relation of law and morality.

The Legal Enforcement of Morality

The preceding discussion of law and morality provides a new way of examining the legal enforcement of morals. As stated earlier, it seems clear that the law always enforces some view of morality. The question is one of guidelines to direct the appropriate use of law. Where morality asks, What ought one to do? law is concerned with a specific subset of that question: When ought the coercive power of the state be used in attempts to enforce the answer to the first question?

Several alternatives are before us as answers to this question. For

John Stuart Mill the only legitimate purpose that can be served through legal coercion of citizens is to prevent harm to others. Devlin states that practices which are "injurious to society" or "harmful to the social fabric" are appropriate targets for legal sanctions. Moving from the proposition that a society cannot exist without morals, he concludes that a society is justified in using legal force to maintain the common morality.[27] Hart, in the reprinted selection from *Law, Liberty, and Morality*, points to a shift in these two approaches by Devlin: a "moderate thesis" which outlaws behavior that harms society, and an "extreme thesis" which implies that the enforcement of the common morality is a thing of value in itself, without a demonstration of harm.[28] In this regard, Hart accuses Devlin of confusing the two senses of "morality," descriptive and judgmental, identified earlier in this essay: "He [Devlin] appears to move from the acceptable position that *some* shared morality is essential to the existence of any society [descriptive] to the unacceptable proposition that a society is identical with its morality as that is at any given moment in its history [judgmental]."[29]

Hart's own position is that any prohibitive practice must result in a substantial enough harm to offset the cost in human misery which legal enforcement entails. Hart does part company with Mill in that he thinks there may be grounds justifying legal coercion other than the prevention of harm to others.[30] Frederick Carney's essay advances the thesis that religious beliefs play a major role in the way people interpret and respond to the legal enforcement of morals. Judgments about the legislation of morality that are grounded in authentic Western faith, he concludes, will be guided by a concern for "the avoidance of harm to human beings and for the protection and development of their interests."[31]

In each case we are presented with a standard by which to evaluate the legitimacy of an effort to prohibit certain activities: harm to others, injury to society, protection and development of human interests. Two major types of problems, however, are encountered when an attempt is made to apply such a standard. First, other values are at work in the decision process. We clearly do not create legal sanctions for all acts which, for example, harm others. The extent of injury, the cost of enforcement, the relationship between the persons involved, the state of mind of the actor, provocation, and a host of other aggravating and mitigating factors come into play. While the essays in this book focus on an important rule, real life judgments have more of the character of responding to a wide array of values, concerns, and beliefs, rather than mechanically applying a formal test based on such a standard.

Second, there is the important issue of determining what such standards mean. How do we decide whether a practice under consideration is harmful to society or contrary to human interests? This is a question, involving process and substance, which is fundamentally a moral question. Ronald Dworkin, in his essay "Lord Devlin and the Enforcement of Morals,"[32] offers some help in moving the discussion to this level.

Dworkin distinguishes between using "moral" in an anthropological sense—referring to any set of attitudes about the propriety of human conduct, qualities, or goals—and using "moral" in a discriminatory sense—contrasting the position being described with prejudices, rationalizations, matters of personal taste, or arbitrary stands.[33] The distinction points to the difference between, on one hand, positions we respect while disagreeing with them and, on the other hand, those we do not respect because they offend our sense of proper moral reasoning.

When advocating the prohibition of a particular practice, argues Dworkin, we must present a position that is moral in this discriminatory sense. We must give morally respectable reasons for the use of legal sanctions. Such reasons exclude postures of judgment based on prejudice. They exclude emotional reactions, positions based on incorrect facts, or a parroting of the beliefs of others. Sincerity and consistency are hallmarks of (discriminatory) moral positions.

The distinction Dworkin draws is an important one for our discussion. His delineation of legitimate and illegitimate grounds for argument clarifies the nature of what often passes for political and moral discourse in our society. At bottom, however, he has not removed the need for debating the substance of differing moral judgments. He has articulated another level at which such disagreements can and should take place. What counts as a prejudiced response to segregation varies from one century to another. What is recognized as an emotional response to homosexuality is different in one decade than in another. This is not to imply that what we now clearly see as inappropriate legislation in years past was right at that time. The point is, rather, that the reasons that pass as morally respectable reasons will change from one social context to another.

Just as we saw earlier that judgments about what is moral or immoral are relational, so are judgments about which arguments merit our respect. Dworkin recognizes this as he sets the community's morality apart from a popular expression of a moral consensus:

> The principles of democracy we follow do not call for the enforcement of the consensus, for the belief that prejudices, personal aversions and rationalizations do not justify restricting another's freedom itself occupies a critical and fundamental position in our popular morality. Nor would the bulk of the community then be entitled to follow its own lights, for the community does not extend that privilege to one who acts on the basis of prejudice, rationalization or personal aversion.[34]

Applied to Devlin's position, Dworkin's statement here presents a case for limiting the enforcement of morals because the enforcement would violate the nature of the society we would be enforcing morals to protect. In the end, this appeal to the community's fundamental morality is the ground for legitimating any legal enforcement of morals. A relational understanding of law and value does not give us any other choices. Whether we are talking about what is moral or immoral, what is harmful, or which reasons deserve respect, we are always left with judgments that are meaningful within a particular social context.

Limiting justifications of legal enforcements of morality to appeals to the community's morality does not, of course, dictate which interpretation of the community's morality we must use. Disagreements about the character of this common moral base are central to contesting which legal sanctions are appropriate. We each come to the debate with our own perspectives, experiences, interests, values, and positions in society—all of which affect the way we interpret our corporate norms. A defender of Mill's position would argue, for example, that individual liberty occupies such a prominent place in our societal morality that it should be abridged only to avoid harm to others. Devlin's approach, on the other hand, sees the maintenance of order through conformity as essential to our community morality and thus justifies a broader range of legal restraints on individuals.

The relational approach to law and morality assumes that these disagreements about the core of societal morality will take place. Just as there are no objective moral absolutes, and just as there is no law existing as a thing in itself, apart from value-laden interpretation, so there is no such thing as *the* community's morality which can be captured in a single, correct statement by an ideal observer. Further, while relational theory restricts discussions of legitimizing legal enforcements of morality to appeal to this common moral base, this approach does not mandate that each citizen unreflectively obey the laws that emerge from such a process.

Moral Objections to Law

The issue of the legal enforcement of morality is concerned with those aspects of morality which can be legitimately enforced by legal sanctions. That issue is quite distinct from decisions by citizens to obey or disobey those laws. While the first issue focuses on the common morality of a particular society, the questions of obedience can be answered in a relational context that is either narrower or broader than the societal context. We make decisions about how to respond to a law as we determine which response is appropriate within different defined relational settings.

Michael Walzer's "The Obligation to Disobey the Law," in the third section of this volume, analyzes disobedience in a way that, at least implicitly, recognizes the relational nature of moral decisions. The duty to disobey, he writes, "arises when obligations incurred in some small group come into conflict with obligations incurred in a larger, more inclusive group, generally the state."[35] As citizens, one way in which we decide what we ought to do is to respond to our interpretation of the law and decide upon an appropriate response as we anticipate further response from the representatives of the state. But we are also members of families, religious organizations, and voluntary associations; we are neighbors, friends, employees, and participants in other groups. In each of these contexts, we respond to values and commitments other than the law, and we anticipate the responses of important persons other than representatives of the state.

Thus, I may disobey a law because a contrary action appears to be more fitting in a smaller context. Without challenging the validity of a 30 MPH speed limit, I may choose to drive much faster to get my injured child to an emergency room. I may participate in an illegal demonstration to call attention to the plight of powerless victims, or to express a sense of solidarity with a group of companions, without questioning whether the law requiring a permit for such activities is legitimate. In these types of cases, I may judge that the values of the more immediate group override those enforced, even legitimately, by the state, and know all the while what the consequences of this disobedience may be.

A second way in which we decide to disobey the law is to conclude that a law is based on an improper interpretation of the community's morality. The conflict is not between acts that are appropriate in different contexts, but between divergent views of what the societal moral consensus means—particularly in relation to what the law ought to be.

Martin Luther King, Jr., in his "Letter from Birmingham City Jail," refers to this national context as he builds his case for civil disobedience:

> We are caught in an inescapable network of mutuality tied in a single garment of destiny. Whatever affects one directly affects all indirectly. . . . Anyone who lives inside the United States can never be considered an outsider anywhere in this country.

> We will reach the goal of freedom in Birmingham and all over the nation, because the goal of America is freedom. Abused and scorned though we may be, our destiny is tied up with the destiny of America.[36]

This letter criticizes Alabama's legislative process as contradictory to the country's democratic tradition. King writes of laying their case before the national conscience and exposing these unjust laws to the light of national opinion. Clearly he believes that these laws should be disobeyed because they do not reflect the societal moral consensus upon which the laws of the United States ought to be based.

King's referential context, however, does have a dual focus: "We will win our freedom because the sacred heritage of our nation and the eternal will of God are embodied in our echoing demands."[37] He expands the relational setting within which he makes his case to include realities and values that transcend the national community. He argues that we have a moral responsibility to obey just laws, and a moral responsibility to disobey unjust laws:

> A just law is a man-made code that squares with the moral law or the law of God. An unjust law is a code that is out of harmony with the moral law. . . . An unjust law is a human law that is not rooted in external and natural law. Any law that uplifts human personality is just. Any law that degrades human personality is unjust.[38]

In this view, appeal is made to a community which is not confined to the borders of the United States: Socrates, Augustine, Aquinas, Martin Buber, Paul Tillich, Jesus, the Christian church. The objects of loyalty, the articles of faith, range beyond democracy and America's destiny to include justice, love, the dignity and worth of human beings, and the will of God. For King there is no fundamental conflict between the national vision and the religious vision. Thus, both contexts are appropriate for advancing a view of what the law ought to be.

This third kind of relational reference, this determination of what is appropriate in light of realities and values that transcend the nation, can lead to disobedience in another way. Transcendent values can focus not only on what the law ought to be, but also on what the community's moral consensus ought to be. Elements of this approach are found in the postwar exchange of letters between Emil Brunner and Karl Barth.

While these two theologians came to different conclusions about the fitting response of Christians to Communism, they base their reasoning on common sources. Brunner writes unabashedly as a member of the Christian church. His opposition to totalitarian regimes is grounded in his judgment that they are intrinsically godless, atheistic, and antitheistic.[39] At no point does this theologian talk about the contradiction between totalitarianism and the heritage of the German nation in the Nazi period, or between Communist regimes and the moral sensibilities of the peoples of Eastern Europe. The point is not that he believes there are no such contradictions, but that for his purposes the "actual" societal moralities are irrelevant. He is working in a broader context, with a determination of appropriate response which would entail both a resistance to these regimes and an advocacy for change in any community morality which did not require this same response.

Barth's field of vision is similar to Brunner's. The response of Christians and the church should be made "in the light of the Word of God and of the Faith."[40] But his judgment about the stance the church takes toward totalitarian regimes is integrally related to the condition of the community's faith and morality. He saw in "Hitler's spell" a spiritual danger, a spiritual source of temptation. National Socialism was a power to overwhelm their souls: "We were in danger of bringing, first incense, and then the complete sacrifice to it as to a false god."[41] This same danger, in Barth's opinion, was not part of the Communist threat. He did not find people who felt this "monster" was a temptation or an enticement, who felt that they were in danger of condoning its deeds or cooperating with it.[42] Barth is, in essence, removing questions of resistance from the transcendent context and referring them back to the more limited relational field of the national community— unless "a definite spiritual crisis were again to develop as it did during the years of 1933–45."[43] Within this approach, it seems that the role of his basic faith, at least in relation to the law, is to keep a society's morality on track so that the community's moral consensus can provide the critical perspective on the law.

The readings in the third section thus give us three alternative models of how decisions about obedience to law are made within a relational approach. Each of these involves deciding upon the fitting action in the midst of different contexts which yield different senses of our responsibilities. The first model presents the possibility of an action viewed as fitting within a smaller group taking precedence over the action that is deemed to be appropriate in the context of a given political jurisdiction. The second model involves conflicts of interpretations of the substance of the community's morality, and therefore a contrary view of what the law ought to be. The third model takes into account our loyalties to principles, communities, traditions, and values which transcend the national scene. It is entirely possible that our determination of what is proper in this larger context can require us to refuse to honor the legal commitments imposed upon us by particular political entities.

Conclusion

We make decisions and we act upon those decisions as we respond to our interpretation of the world in which we live. This response takes account of the anticipated response of significant others to our action. The interpreting, the anticipating, the defining of the significant community, and the final determination of what response is appropriate are all shaped by the causes to which we are committed, and the values to which we are faithful. These, in turn, are rooted in a fundamental faith—an affirmation of that reality or realities to which we give our ultimate loyalty.

This description of the structure of human action is as valid for decisions made in a legal context as for those made in familial, religious, economic, political, or other relational contexts. The overarching moral question is, What ought I to do? The law is one aspect of the world to which we respond, and thus legal considerations are a part of the total range of considerations that feed into the decision-making process.

This view of the legal sphere as inevitably related to the moral process does not deny the distinctiveness of law. When law is a factor in making the normative decision, our response is demanded to certain "legal" realities: for example, statutes, judicial decisions, administrative regulations. Our interpretation of those realities is properly colored by another distinctive set of factors: principles of civil rights, constitutional provisions, legislative intent, attorney's advice, and views of what the law ought to be in light of the community's moral heritage. The anticipation of response from a specified set of actors comes into play: police officers, prosecutors, judges, juries, legislators, fellow citizens. The law has meaning as law not because it is coercive (many nonlegal sanctions are coercive), or because it has been decreed by constituted authority (consider the provision on the books that is universally ignored), but because it is treated as law. Law is identified by the nature of the realities to which we are responding, the interpretative framework that is germane to understanding those realities, and the community of significant others whose response is anticipated.

While the arena of legal decision making is distinctive, it is not isolated from the larger moral world. Our judgments about when we should disobey the law, about which parts of our morality should be subject to legal sanction, and even about what the law is, are all made within our moral perspectives that have been formed in relation to causes, values, and "truths" other than those that are "legal." Thus, rather than speaking of law and morality as two discrete realities, we should speak of the moral dimension of law, a dimension that is revealed when any legal inquiry is pushed far enough.

NOTES

1. H. L. A. Hart, *Law, Liberty, and Morality* (Stanford, Calif.: Stanford University Press, 1963) 2.

2. The Hon. Sir Patrick Devlin, *The Enforcement of Morals* (London: Oxford University Press, 1965) 4.

3. Devlin, *The Enforcement of Morals;* Hart, *Law, Liberty, and Morality.* The first remarks were made by Devlin in the Maccabaean Lecture in Jurisprudence of the British Academy, 1959. Hart's response came in the Harry Camp Lectures at Stanford University three years later. Hart phrased the question as follows: "Is the fact that certain conduct is by common standards immoral sufficient to justify making that conduct punishable by law?"

4. John Stuart Mill, *On Liberty* (Gateway ed.; Chicago: Henry Regnery Co., 1955) 13; first published in 1859.

5. H. L. A. Hart, "Positivism and the Separation of Law and Morals," *Harvard Law Review* 71 (1958) 593–629; Lon L. Fuller, "Positivism and Fidelity to Law—A Reply to Professor Hart," *Harvard Law Review* 71 (1958) 630–72.

6. Thomas Aquinas, *The Summa Theologica,* Part One of the Second Part, Question 93, Third Article.

7. William Blackstone, *Blackstone's Commentaries,* vol. 1 (ed. St. George Tucker; London: Augustus M. Kelley, 1969) 41; first published in 1803. The last phrase of this passage raises a second concern. While saying that laws are

not valid unless they conform to the law of nature, Blackstone also asserts that any valid law derives its authority from this divine source. The first proposition supplies a critical principle for invalidating laws. The second proposition gives a supernatural warrant to any law which is considered valid and, by implication, asserts that legal and moral obligation coincide.

8. See p. 148 below.

9. John Austin, *The Province of Jurisprudence Determined* (Library of Ideas ed., 1954) 184; first published, London: Weidenfeld & Nicolson, 1832.

10. Hart, "Positivism," 600.

11. Hans Kelsen, *General Theory of Law and State* (trans. Anders Wedberg; Cambridge, Mass.: Harvard University Press, 1945) 113.

12. David A. J. Richards, *The Moral Criticism of Law* (Encino, Calif.: Dickenson Publishing Company, 1977) 178.

13. Richards, *Moral Criticism,* 265.

14. H. L. A. Hart, *The Concept of Law* (Oxford: Clarendon Press, 1961) 113.

15. Hart, *Law, Liberty, and Morality,* 2.

16. An exception to this appears to be Hans Kelsen's "pure" theory of law as he speaks of a conflict between a norm of positive law and a norm of morality: "Two norms which by their significance contradict and hence logically exclude one another, cannot be simultaneously assumed to be valid" (*General Theory,* 375).

17. H. Richard Niebuhr, *The Responsible Self* (New York: Harper & Row, 1963). The following discussion of approaches to understanding the moral life borrows heavily from chapter 1, pp. 47–68.

18. Ibid., 61–65.

19. H. Richard Niebuhr, "The Center of Value," in *Radical Monotheism and Western Culture* (New York: Harper & Row, 1960) 100–113.

20. Douglas Sturm, "Three Contexts of Law," *Journal of Religion* 47 (1964) 136–37.

21. Ibid., 136.

22. For example, in *Church of the Holy Trinity* v. *U.S.,* the U.S. Supreme Court held that "General terms should be so limited in their application as not to lead to injustice, oppression or an absurd consequence." 143 U.S. 457 (1892), quoting from the opinion in *U.S.* v. *Kirby,* 7 Wall. 482, 486.

23. R. M. Unger, "The Critical Legal Studies Movement," *Harvard Law Review* 96 (1983) 564. In this sweeping presentation of the Critical Legal Studies Movement, Unger argues that attempts to maintain a contrast between legal analysis and ideological conflict reduce legal doctrine to a "series of seemingly dogmatic assumptions and arbitrary distinctions" (p. 611).

24. Harold Berman, *The Interaction of Law and Religion* (Nashville: Abingdon Press, 1974) 24.

25. Steven J. Burton casts this contextual process in a slightly different way: "The judge does not decide a case by confronting the facts with a single rule or precedent in mind or with wholly personal value preferences. The judge confronts a case in a light of a web of beliefs about what members of the legal community generally will take to be required by an orderly and just

society in a case or like cases, as indicated by the legal experience and the totality of our theories about law" (*An Introduction to Law and Legal Reasoning* [Boston: Little, Brown & Co., 1985] 143).

26. Stanley Fish, "Fish v. Fiss," *Stanford Law Review* 36 (1984) 1328. A professor of English, Fish has made a major contribution to legal scholarship through his application of the methods of literary criticism to law.

27. Devlin, *The Enforcement of Morals*, 12–3, 25.

28. Hart, *Law, Liberty, and Morality,* 48–50.

29. Ibid., 51.

30. Ibid., 5. While Hart does not state which grounds he would endorse, Carney has identified some reasons that are at least presented for consideration by Hart. See Frederick S. Carney, "Religion and the Legislation of Morals" *Soundings* 51 (1968) 434.

31. Carney, 444.

32. Ronald Dworkin, "Lord Devlin and the Enforcement of Morals," *Yale Law Journal* 75 (1966) 986–1005.

33. Ibid., 994. The anthropological/discriminatory distinction is not the same as the descriptive/judgmental distinction used earlier in this essay. Dworkin's use of "moral" in a discriminatory sense does not imply approval of the substance of a position; it implies simply "respect" for the grounding of the position.

34. Ibid., 1001.

35. Michael Walzer, *Obligations: Essays on Disobedience, War, and Citizenship* (Cambridge: Harvard University Press, 1970) 10.

36. See pp. 144, 156 below.

37. See p. 156 below.

38. See p. 148 below.

39. Emil Brunner, "An Open Letter to Karl Barth," in *Against the Stream* (New York: Philosophical Library, 1954) 110.

40. Karl Barth, "Karl Barth's Reply," in *Against the Stream,* 114.

41. Ibid., 115.

42. Ibid., 116.

43. Ibid., 117.

PART ONE

THE LEGAL ENFORCEMENT
OF MORALITY

1

*Morals and the Criminal Law**

Lord Patrick Devlin

The Report of the Committee on Homosexual Offenses and Prostitution, generally known as the Wolfenden Report, is recognized to be an excellent study of two very difficult legal and social problems. But it has also a particular claim to the respect of those interested in jurisprudence; it does what law reformers so rarely do; it sets out clearly and carefully what in relation to its subjects it considers the function of the law to be. Statutory additions to the criminal law are too often made on the simple principle that "there ought to be a law against it." The greater part of the law relating to sexual offenses is the creation of statute and it is difficult to ascertain any logical relationship between it and the moral ideas which most of us uphold. Adultery, fornication, and prostitution are not, as the Report[1] points out, criminal offenses: homosexuality between males is a criminal offense, but between females it is not. Incest was not an offense until it was declared so by statute only fifty years ago. Does the legislature select these offenses haphazardly or are there some principles which can be used to determine what part of the moral law should be embodied in the criminal? There is, for example, being now considered a proposal to make A.I.D., that is, the practice of artificial insemination of a woman with the seed of a man who is not her husband, a criminal offense; if, as is usually the case, the woman is

*Maccabaean Lecture in Jurisprudence read at the British Academy on 18 March 1959 and printed in *Proceedings of the British Acedamy* 45 under the title "The Enforcement of Morals." Republished in *The Enforcement of Morals* by Lord Patrick Devlin (1965) 1–25.

married, this is in substance, if not in form, adultery. Ought it to be made punishable when adultery is not? This sort of question is of practical importance, for a law that appears to be arbitrary and illogical, in the end and after the wave of moral indignation that has put it on the statute book subsides, forfeits respect. As a practical question it arises more frequently in the field of sexual morals than in any other, but there is no special answer to be found in that field. The inquiry must be general and fundamental. What is the connection between crime and sin and to what extent, if at all, should the criminal law of England concern itself with the enforcement of morals and punish sin or immorality as such? . . .

There are many schools of thought among those who may think that morals are not the law's business. There is first of all the agnostic or free-thinker. He does not of course disbelieve in morals, nor in sin if it be given the wider of the two meanings assigned to it in the *Oxford English Dictionary* where it is defined as "transgression against divine law or the principles of morality." He cannot accept the divine law; that does not mean that he might not view with suspicion any departure from moral principles that have for generations been accepted by the society in which he lives; but in the end he judges for himself. Then there is the deeply religious person who feels that the criminal law is sometimes more of a hindrance than a help in the sphere of morality, and that the reform of the sinner—at any rate when he injures only himself—should be a spiritual rather than a temporal work. Then there is the man who without any strong feeling cannot see why, where there is freedom in religious belief, there should not logically be freedom in morality as well. All these are powerfully allied against the equating of crime with sin. . . .

Morals and religion are inextricably joined—the moral standards generally accepted in Western civilization being those belonging to Christianity. Outside Christendom other standards derive from other religions. None of these moral codes can claim any validity except by virtue of the religion on which it is based. Old Testament morals differ in some respects from New Testament morals. Even within Christianity there are differences. Some hold that contraception is an immoral practice and that a man who has carnal knowledge of another woman while his wife is alive is in all circumstances a fornicator; others, including most of the English-speaking world, deny both these propositions. Between the great religions of the world, of which Christianity is only one, there are much wider differences. It may or may not be right for the State to adopt one of these religions as the truth, to found itself upon its doctrines, and to deny to any of its citizens the liberty to practice any other. If it does, it is logical that it should use the secular law wherever it thinks it necessary to enforce the divine. If it does not, it is illogical that it should concern itself with morals as such. But if it leaves matters of religion to private judgment, it should logically leave matters of morals also. A State which refuses to enforce Christian beliefs has lost the right to enforce Christian morals.

If this view is sound, it means that the criminal law cannot justify any of its provisions by reference to the moral law. It cannot say, for example, that murder and theft are prohibited because they are immoral or sinful. The State must justify in some other way the punishments which it imposes on wrongdoers and a function for the criminal law independent of morals must be found. This is not difficult to do. The smooth functioning of society and the preservation of order require that a number of activities should be regulated. The rules that are made for that purpose and are enforced by the criminal law are often designed simply to achieve uniformity and convenience and rarely involve any choice between good and evil. Rules that impose a speed limit or prevent obstruction on the highway have nothing to do with morals. Since so much of the criminal law is composed of rules of this sort, why bring morals into it at all? Why not define the function of the criminal law in simple terms as the preservation of order and decency and the protection of the lives and property of citizens, and elaborate those terms in relation to any particular subject in the way in which it is done in the Wolfenden Report? . . .

I think it is clear that the criminal law as we know it is based upon moral principle. In a number of crimes its function is simply to enforce a moral principle and nothing else. The law, both criminal and civil, claims to be able to speak about morality and immorality generally. Where does it get its authority to do this and how does it settle the moral principles which it enforces? Undoubtedly, as a matter of history, it derived both from Christian teaching. But I think that the strict logician is right when he says that the law can no longer rely on doctrines in which citizens are entitled to disbelieve. It is necessary therefore to look for some other source.

In jurisprudence, as I have said, everything is thrown open to discussion and, in the belief that they cover the whole field, I have framed three interrogatories addressed to myself to answer:

1. Has society the right to pass judgment at all on matters of morals? Ought there, in other words, to be a public morality, or are morals always a matter for private judgment?

2. If society has the right to pass judgment, has it also the right to use the weapon of the law to enforce it?
3. If so, ought it to use that weapon in all cases or only in some; and if only in some, on what principles should it distinguish?

I shall begin with the first interrogatory and consider what is meant by the right of society to pass a moral judgment, that is, a judgment about what is good and what is evil. The fact that a majority of people may disapprove of a practice does not of itself make it a matter for society as a whole. Nine men out of ten may disapprove of what the tenth man is doing and still say that it is not their business. There is a case for a collective judgment (as distinct from a large number of individual opinions which sensible people may even refrain from pronouncing at all if it is upon somebody else's private affairs) only if society is affected. Without a collective judgment there can be no case at all for intervention. . . .

What makes a society of any sort is community of ideas, not only political ideas but also ideas about the way its members should behave and govern their lives; these latter ideas are its morals. Every society has a moral structure as well as a political one: or rather, since that might suggest two independent systems, I should say that the structure of every society is made up both of politics and morals. Take, for example, the institution of marriage. Whether a man should be allowed to take more than one wife is something about which every society has to make up its mind one way or the other. In England we believe in the Christian idea of marriage and therefore adopt monogamy as a moral principle. Consequently the Christian institution of marriage has become the basis of family life and so part of the structure of our society. It is there not because it is Christian. It has got there because it is Christian, but it remains there because it is built into the house in which we live and could not be removed without bringing it down. The great majority of those who live in this country accept it because it is the Christian idea of marriage and for them the only true one. But a non-Christian is bound by it, not because it is part of Christianity but because, rightly or wrongly, it has been adopted by the society in which he lives. It would be useless for him to stage a debate designed to prove that polygamy was theologically more correct and socially preferable; if he wants to live in the house, he must accept it as built in the way in which it is.

We see this more clearly if we think of ideas or institutions that are purely political. Society cannot tolerate rebellion; it will not allow argument about the rightness of the cause. Historians a century later may say that the rebels were right and the government was wrong and a percipient and conscientious subject of the State may think so at the time. But it is not a matter which can be left to individual judgment.

The institution of marriage is a good example for my purpose because it bridges the division, if there is one, between politics and morals. Marriage is part of the structure of our society and it is also the basis of a moral code which condemns fornication and adultery. The institution of marriage would be gravely threatened if individual judgments were permitted about the morality of adultery; on these points there must be a public morality. But public morality is not to be confined to those moral principles which support institutions such as marriage. People do not think of monogamy as something which has to be supported because our society has chosen to organize itself upon it; they think of it as something that is good in itself and offering a good way of life and that it is for that reason that our society has adopted it. I return to the statement that I have already made, that society means a community of ideas; without shared ideas on politics, morals, and ethics no society can exist. Each one of us has ideas about what is good and what is evil; they cannot be kept private from the society in which we live. If men and women try to create a society in which there is no fundamental agreement about good and evil they will fail; if, having based it on common agreement, the agreement goes, the society will disintegrate. . . .

You may think that I have taken far too long in contending that there is such a thing as public morality, a proposition which most people would readily accept, and may have left myself too little time to discuss the next question which to many minds may cause greater difficulty: to what extent should society use the law to enforce its moral judgments? But I believe that the answer to the first question determines the way in which the second should be approached and may indeed very nearly dictate the answer to the second question. If society has no right to make judgments on morals, the law must find some special justification for entering the field of morality: if homosexuality and prostitution are not in themselves wrong, then the onus is very clearly on the lawgiver who wants to frame a law against certain aspects of them to justify the exceptional treatment. But if society has the right to make a judgment and has it on the basis that a recognized morality is as necessary to society as, say, a recognized government, then society may use the law to preserve morality in the same way as it uses it to safeguard anything else that is essential to its existence. If therefore the first proposition is securely established with all its implications, society has a prima facie right to legislate against immorality as such. . . .

Society is entitled by means of its laws to protect itself from dangers, whether from within or without. Here again I think that the political parallel is legitimate. The law of treason is directed against aiding the king's enemies and against sedition from within. The justification for this is that established government is necessary for the existence of society and therefore its safety against violent overthrow must be secured. But an established morality is as necessary as good government to the welfare of society. Societies disintegrate from within more frequently than they are broken up by external pressures. There is disintegration when no common morality is observed and history shows that the loosening of moral bonds is often the first stage of disintegration, so that society is justified in taking the same steps to preserve its moral code as it does to preserve its government and other essential institutions.[2] The suppression of vice is as much the law's business as the suppression of subversive activities; it is no more possible to define a sphere of private morality than it is to define one of private subversive activity. It is wrong to talk of private morality or of the law not being concerned with immorality as such or to try to set rigid bounds to the part which the law may play in the suppression of vice. There are no theoretical limits to the power of the State to legislate against treason and sedition, and likewise I think there can be no theoretical limits to legislation against immorality. You may argue that if a man's sins affect only himself it cannot be the concern of society. If he chooses to get drunk every night in the privacy of his own home, is anyone except himself the worse for it? But suppose a quarter or a half of the population got drunk every night, what sort of society would it be? You cannot set a theoretical limit to the number of people who can get drunk before society is entitled to legislate against drunkenness. The same may be said of gambling. The Royal Commission on Betting, Lotteries, and Gaming took as their test the character of the citizen as a member of society. They said: "Our concern with the ethical significance of gambling is confined to the effect which it may have on the character of the gambler as a member of society. If we were convinced that whatever the degree of gambling this effect must be harmful we should be inclined to think that it was the duty of the state to restrict gambling to the greatest extent practicable."[3]

In what circumstances the State should exercise its power is the third of the interrogatories I have framed. But before I get to it I must raise a point which might have been brought up in any one of the three. How are the moral judgments of society to be ascertained? By leaving it until now, I can ask it in the more limited form that is now sufficient for my purpose. How is the law-maker to ascertain the moral judgments of society? It is surely not enough that they should be reached by the opinion of the majority; it would be too much to require the individual assent of every citizen. English law has evolved and regularly uses a standard which does not depend on the counting of heads. It is that of the reasonable man. He is not to be confused with the rational man. He is not expected to reason about anything and his judgment may be largely a matter of feeling. It is the view-point of the man in the street—or to use an archaism familiar to all lawyers—the man in the Clapham omnibus. He might also be called the right-minded man. For my purpose I should like to call him the man in the jury box, for the moral judgment of society must be something about which any twelve men or women drawn at random might after discussion be expected to be unanimous. This was the standard the judges applied in the days before Parliament was as active as it is now and when they laid down rules of public policy. They did not think of themselves as making law but simply as stating principles which every right-minded person would accept as valid. . . .

Nothing should be punished by the law that does not lie beyond the limits of tolerance. It is not nearly enough to say that a majority dislike a practice; there must be a real feeling of reprobation. Those who are dissatisfied with the present law on homosexuality often say that the opponents of reform are swayed simply by disgust. If that were so it would be wrong, but I do not think one can ignore disgust if it is deeply felt and not manufactured. Its presence is a good indication that the bounds of toleration are being reached. Not everything is to be tolerated. No society can do without intolerance, indignation, and disgust; they are the forces behind the moral law, and indeed it can be argued that if they or something like them are not present, the feelings of society cannot be weighty enough to deprive the individual of freedom of choice. I suppose that there is hardly anyone nowadays who would not be disgusted by the thought of deliberate cruelty to animals. No one proposes to relegate that or any other form of sadism to the realm of private morality or to allow it to be practiced in public or in private. It would be possible no doubt to point out that until a comparatively short while ago nobody thought very much of cruelty to animals and also that pity and kindliness and the unwillingness to inflict pain are virtues more generally esteemed now than they have ever been in the past. But matters of this sort are not determined by rational argument. Every moral judgment, unless it claims a divine source, is simply a feeling that no right-minded man could behave in any other way without admitting that he was doing wrong. It is the power of a common sense and not the power of reason that is behind the judgments of society. But before a society can put a practice beyond the limits of tolerance there must be a deliberate judgment that the practice is injurious to society. There is, for example, a general abhorrence of homosexuality. We should ask ourselves in the first instance whether, looking at it calmly and dispassionately, we regard it as a vice so abominable that its mere presence is an offense. If that is the genuine feeling of the society in which we live, I do not see how society can be denied the right to eradicate it. Our feeling may not be so intense as that. We may feel about it that, if confined, it is tolerable, but that if it spread it might be gravely injurious; it is in this way that most societies look upon fornication, seeing it as a natural weakness which must be kept within bounds but which cannot be rooted out. It becomes then a question of balance, the danger to society in one scale and the extent of the restriction in the other. On this sort of point the value of an investigation by such a body as the Wolfenden Committee and of its conclusions is manifest.

The limits of tolerance shift. This is supplementary to what I have been saying but of sufficient importance in itself to deserve statement as a separate principle which law-makers have to bear in mind. I suppose that moral standards do not shift; so far as they come from divine revelation they do not, and I am willing to assume that the moral judgments made by a society always remain good for that society. But the extent to which society will tolerate—I mean tolerate, not approve—departures from moral standards varies from generation to generation. . . .

It follows as another good working principle that in any new matter of morals the law should be slow to act. By the next generation the swell of indignation may have abated and the law be left without the strong backing which it needs. But it is then difficult to alter the law without giving the impression that moral judgment is being weakened. This is now one of the factors that is strongly militating against any alteration to the law on homosexuality.

A third elastic principle must be advanced more tentatively. It is that as far as possible privacy should be respected. This is not an

idea that has ever been made explicit in the criminal law. Acts or
words done or said in public or in private are all brought within its
scope without distinction in principle. But there goes with this a
strong reluctance on the part of judges and legislators to sanction
invasions of privacy in the detection of crime. The police have no
more right to trespass than the ordinary citizen has; there is no general right of search; to this extent an Englishman's home is still his
castle. . . .

The last and the biggest thing to be remembered is that the law is
concerned with the minimum and not with the maximum; there
is much in the Sermon on the Mount that would be out of place in
the Ten Commandments. We all recognize the gap between the
moral law and the law of the land. No man is worth much who
regulates his conduct with the sole object of escaping punishment,
and every worthy society sets for its members standards which are
above those of the law. We recognize the existence of such higher
standards when we use expressions such as "moral obligation" and
"morally bound." . . .

The line that divides the criminal law from the moral is not deter-
minable by the application of any clear-cut principle. It is like a line
that divides land and sea, a coastline of irregularities and indenta-
tions. There are gaps and promontories, such as adultery and fornication, which the law has for centuries left substantially untouched.
Adultery of the sort that breaks up marriage seems to me to be just as
harmful to the social fabric as homosexuality or bigamy. The only
ground for putting it outside the criminal law is that a law which
made it a crime would be too difficult to enforce; it is too generally
regarded as a human weakness not suitably punished by imprisonment. All that the law can do with fornication is to act against its
worst manifestations; there is a general abhorrence of the commer-
cialization of vice, and that sentiment gives strength to the law
against brothels and immoral earnings. There is no logic to be found
in this. The boundary between the criminal law and the moral law is
fixed by balancing in the case of each particular crime the pros and
cons of legal enforcement in accordance with the sort of considerations I have been outlining. The fact that adultery, fornication, and
lesbianism are untouched by the criminal law does not prove that
homosexuality ought not to be touched. The error of jurisprudence
in the Wolfenden Report is caused by the search for some single
principle to explain the division between crime and sin. The Report
finds it in the principle that the criminal law exists for the protection

of individuals; on this principle fornication in private between consenting adults is outside the law and thus it becomes logically indefensible to bring homosexuality between consenting adults in private within it. But the true principle is that the law exists for the protection of society. It does not discharge its function by protecting the individual from injury, annoyance, corruption, and exploitation; the law must protect also the institutions and the community of ideas, political and moral, without which people cannot live together. Society cannot ignore the morality of the individual any more than it can his loyalty; it flourishes on both and without either it dies.

I have said that the morals which underly the law must be derived from the sense of right and wrong which resides in the community as a whole; it does not matter whence the community of thought comes, whether from one body of doctrine or another or from the knowledge of good and evil which no man is without. If the reasonable man believes that a practice is immoral and believes also—no matter whether the belief is right or wrong, so be it that it is honest and dispassionate—that no right-minded member of his society could think otherwise, then for the purpose of the law it is immoral. This, you may say, makes immorality a question of fact—what the law would consider as self-evident fact no doubt, but still with no higher authority than any other doctrine of public policy. I think that that is so, and indeed the law does not distinguish between an act that is immoral and one that is contrary to public policy. But the law has never yet had occasion to inquire into the differences between Christian morals and those which every right-minded member of society is expected to hold. The inquiry would, I believe, be academic. Moralists would find differences; indeed they would find them between different branches of the Christian faith on subjects such as divorce and birth-control. But for the purpose of the limited entry which the law makes into the field of morals, there is no practical difference. It seems to me therefore that the free-thinker and the non-Christian can accept, without offense to his convictions, the fact that Christian morals are the basis of the criminal law and that he can recognize, also without taking offense, that without the support of the churches the moral order, which has its origin in and takes its strength from Christian beliefs, would collapse.

This brings me back in the end to a question I posed at the beginning. What is the relationship between crime and sin, between the Church and the Law? I do not think that you can equate crime with sin. The divine law and the secular have been disunited, but they are brought together again by the need which each has for the other. It is not my function to emphasize the Church's need of the secular law; it can be put tersely by saying that you cannot have a ceiling without a floor. I am very clear about the Law's need for the Church. I have spoken of the criminal law as dealing with the minimum standards of human conduct and the moral law with the maximum. The instrument of the criminal law is punishment; those of the moral law are teaching, training, and exhortation. If the whole dead weight of sin were ever to be allowed to fall upon the law, it could not take the strain. If at any point there is a lack of clear and convincing moral teaching, the administration of the law suffers. . . .

Society cannot live without morals. Its morals are those standards of conduct which the reasonable man approves. A rational man, who is also a good man, may have other standards. If he has no standards at all he is not a good man and need not be further considered. If he has standards, they may be very different; he may, for example, not disapprove of homosexuality or abortion. In that case he will not share in the common morality; but that should not make him deny that it is a social necessity. A rebel may be rational in thinking that he is right but he is irrational if he thinks that society can leave him free to rebel.

A man who concedes that morality is necessary to society must support the use of those instruments without which morality cannot be maintained. The two instruments are those of teaching, which is doctrine, and of enforcement, which is the law. If morals could be taught simply on the basis that they are necessary to society, there would be no social need for religion; it could be left as a purely personal affair. But morality cannot be taught in that way. Loyalty is not taught in that way either. No society has yet solved the problem of how to teach morality without religion. So the law must base itself on Christian morals and to the limit of its ability enforce them, not simply because they are the morals of most of us, nor simply because they are the morals which are taught by the established Church—on these points the law recognizes the right to dissent—but for the compelling reason that without the help of Christian teaching the law will fail.

NOTES

1. Paragraph 14.
2. It is somewhere about this point in the argument that Professor Hart in *Law, Liberty, and Morality* discerns a proposition which he describes

as central to my thought. He states the proposition and his objection to it as follows (p. 51; p. 48 in this volume): "He appears to move from the acceptable proposition that *some* shared morality is essential to the existence of any society [this I take to be the proposition on p. 12] to the unacceptable proposition that a society is identical with its morality as that is at any given moment of its history, so that a change in its morality is tantamount to the destruction of a society. The former proposition might be even accepted as a necessary rather than an empirical truth depending on a quite plausible definition of society as a body of men who hold certain moral views in common. But the latter proposition is absurd. Taken strictly, it would prevent us saying that the morality of a given society had changed, and would compel us instead to say that one society had disappeared and another one taken its place. But it is only on this absurd criterion of what it is for the same society to continue to exist that it could be asserted without evidence that any deviation from a society's shared morality threatens its existence." In conclusion (p. 82; p. 55 in this volume) Professor Hart condemns the whole thesis in the lecture as based on "a confused definition of what a society is."

I do not assert that *any* deviation from a society's shared morality threatens its existence any more than I assert that *any* subversive activity threatens its existence. I assert that they are both activities which are capable in their nature of threatening the existence of society so that neither can be put beyond the law.

3. (1951) Cmd. 8190, paragraph 159.

2

*Law, Liberty, and Morality**

H. L. A. Hart

The Legal Enforcement of Morality

These lectures are concerned with one question about the relations between law and morals. I say, advisedly, "one question," because in the heat of the controversy often generated when law and morals are mentioned in conjunction, it is often overlooked that there is not just one question concerning their relations but many different questions needing quite separate consideration. . . .

[The "one question"] concerns the legal enforcement of morality and has been formulated in many different ways: Is the fact that certain conduct is by common standards immoral sufficient to justify making that conduct punishable by law? Is it morally permissible to enforce morality as such? Ought immorality as such to be a crime?

To this question John Stuart Mill gave an emphatic negative answer in his essay *On Liberty* one hundred years ago, and the famous sentence in which he frames this answer expresses the central doctrine of his essay. He said, "The only purpose for which power can rightfully be exercised over any member of a civilised community against his will is to prevent harm to others."[1] And to identify the many different things which he intended to exclude, he added, "His own good either physical or moral is not a sufficient warrant. He cannot rightfully be compelled to do or forbear because it will be better for him to do so, because it will make him

*First published as the Harry Camp Lectures (1963) under the title *Law, Liberty, and Morality*.

happier, because in the opinions of others, to do so would be wise or even right."[2]

This doctrine, Mill tells us, is to apply to human beings only "in the maturity of their faculties": it is not to apply to children or to backward societies. Even so, it has been the object of much academic criticism on two different, and indeed inconsistent, grounds. Some critics have urged that the line which Mill attempts to draw between actions with which the law may interfere and those with which it may not is illusory. "No man is an island"; and in an organized society it is impossible to identify classes of actions which harm no one or no one but the individual who does them. Other critics have admitted that such a division of actions may be made, but insist that it is merely dogmatic on Mill's part to limit legal coercion to the class of actions which harm others. There are good reasons, so these critics claim, for compelling conformity to social morality and for punishing deviations from it even when these do not harm others.

I shall consider this dispute mainly in relation to the special topic of sexual morality where it seems prima facie plausible that there are actions immoral by accepted standards and yet not harmful to others. But to prevent misunderstanding I wish to enter a caveat; I do not propose to defend all that Mill said; for I myself think there may be grounds justifying the legal coercion of the individual other than the prevention of harm to others. But on the narrower issue relevant to the enforcement of morality Mill seems to me to be right. . . .

Mill's principles are still very much alive in the criticism of law, whatever their theoretical deficiencies may be. But twice in one hundred years they have been challenged by two masters of the common law. The first of these was the great Victorian judge and historian of the criminal law, James Fitzjames Stephen. His criticism of Mill is to be found in the somber and impressive book *Liberty, Equality, Fraternity,*[3] which he wrote as a direct reply to Mill's essay *On Liberty.* It is evident from the tone of this book that Stephen thought he had found crushing arguments against Mill and had demonstrated that the law might justifiably enforce morality as such or, as he said, that the law should be "a persecution of the grosser forms of vice."[4] Nearly a century later, on the publication of the Wolfenden Committee's report, Lord Devlin, now a member of the House of Lords and a most distinguished writer on the criminal law, in his essay on *The Enforcement of Morals*[5] took as his target the report's contention "that there must be a realm of morality and immorality which is not the law's business" and argued in opposition to it that "the suppression of vice is as much the law's business as the suppression of subversive activities."

Though a century divides these two legal writers, the similarity in the general tone and sometimes in the detail of their arguments is very great. I shall devote the remainder of these lectures to an examination of them. I do this because, though their arguments are at points confused, they certainly still deserve the compliment of rational opposition. They are not only admirably stocked with concrete examples, but they express the considered views of skilled, sophisticated lawyers experienced in the administration of the criminal law. Views such as theirs are still quite widely held especially by lawyers both in England and in this country; it may indeed be that they are more popular, in both countries, than Mill's doctrine of liberty. . . .

Paternalism and the Enforcement of Morality

I shall start with an example stressed by Lord Devlin. He points out[6] that, subject to certain exceptions such as rape, the criminal law has never admitted the consent of the victim as a defense. It is not a defense to a charge of murder or a deliberate assault, and this is why euthanasia or mercy killing terminating a man's life at his own request is still murder. This is a rule of criminal law which many now would wish to retain, though they would also wish to object to the legal punishment of offenses against positive morality which harm no one. Lord Devlin thinks that these attitudes are inconsistent, for he asserts of the rule under discussion, "There is only one explanation," and this is that "there are certain standards of behaviour or moral principles which society requires to be observed."[7] Among these are the sanctity of human life and presumably (since the rule applies to assaults) the physical integrity of the person. So in the case of this rule and a number of others Lord Devlin claims that the "function" of the criminal law is "to enforce a moral principle and nothing else."[8]

But this argument is not really cogent, for Lord Devlin's statement that "there is only one explanation" is simply not true. The rules excluding the victim's consent as a defense to charges of murder or assault may perfectly well be explained as a piece of paternalism, designed to protect individuals against themselves. Mill no doubt might have protested against a paternalistic policy of using the law to protect even a consenting victim from bodily harm nearly as much as he protested against laws used merely to enforce positive morality;

but this does not mean that these two policies are identical. Indeed, Mill himself was very well aware of the difference between them: for in condemning interference with individual liberty except to prevent harm to others he mentions *separate* types of inadequate ground which have been proffered for the use of compulsion. He distinguishes "because it will be better for him" and "because it will make him happier" from "because in the opinion of others it would be right."[9]

Lord Devlin says of the attitude of the criminal law to the victim's consent that if the law existed for the protection of the individual there would be no reason why he should avail himself of it if he did not want it.[10] But paternalism—the protection of people against themselves—is a perfectly coherent policy. Indeed, it seems very strange in mid-twentieth century to insist upon this, for the wane of laissez faire since Mill's day is one of the commonplaces of social history, and instances of paternalism now abound in our law, criminal and civil. The supply of drugs or narcotics, even to adults, except under medical prescription is punishable by the criminal law, and it would seem very dogmatic to say of the law creating this offense that "there is only one explanation," namely, that the law was concerned not with the protection of the would-be purchasers against themselves, but only with the punishment of the seller for his immorality. If, as seems obvious, paternalism is a possible explanation of such laws, it is also possible in the case of the rule excluding the consent of the victim as a defense to a charge of assault. In neither case are we forced to conclude with Lord Devlin that the law's "function" is "to enforce a moral principle and nothing else."[11]

In chapter 5 of his essay Mill carried his protests against paternalism to lengths that may now appear to us fantastic. He cites the example of restrictions of the sale of drugs, and criticizes them as interferences with the liberty of the would-be purchaser rather than with that of the seller. No doubt if we no longer sympathize with this criticism this is due, in part, to a general decline in the belief that individuals know their own interests best, and to an increased awareness of a great range of factors which diminish the significance to be attached to an apparently free choice or to consent. Choices may be made or consent given without adequate reflection or appreciation of the consequences; or in pursuit of merely transitory desires; or in various predicaments when the judgment is likely to be clouded; or under inner psychological compulsion; or under pressure by others of a kind too subtle to be susceptible of proof in a law court. Underlying

Mill's extreme fear of paternalism there perhaps is a conception of what a normal human being is like which now seems not to correspond to the facts. Mill, in fact, endows him with too much of the psychology of a middle-aged man whose desires are relatively fixed, not liable to be artificially stimulated by external influences; who knows what he wants and what gives him satisfaction or happiness; and who pursues these things when he can.

Certainly a modification in Mill's principles is required, if they are to accommodate the rule of criminal law under discussion or other instances of paternalism. But the modified principles would not abandon the objection to the use of the criminal law merely to enforce positive morality. They would only have to provide that harming others is something we may still seek to prevent by use of the criminal law, even when the victims consent to or assist in the acts which are harmful to them. The neglect of the distinction between paternalism and what I have termed legal moralism is important as a form of a more general error. It is too often assumed that if a law is not designed to protect one man from another its only rationale can be that it is designed to punish moral wickedness or, in Lord Devlin's words, "to enforce a moral principle." Thus it is often urged that statutes punishing cruelty to animals can only be explained in that way. But it is certainly intelligible, both as an account of the original motives inspiring such legislation and as the specification of an aim widely held to be worth pursuing, to say that the law is here concerned with the *suffering,* albeit only of animals, rather than with the immorality of torturing them. Certainly no one who supports this use of the criminal law is thereby bound in consistency to admit that the law may punish forms of immorality which involve no suffering to any sentient being. . . .

The Moderate and the
Extreme Thesis

When we turn from these examples which are certainly disputable to the positive grounds held to justify the legal enforcement of morality it is important to distinguish a moderate and an extreme thesis, though critics of Mill have sometimes moved from one to the other without marking the transition. Lord Devlin seems to me to maintain, for most of his essay, the moderate thesis and Stephen the extreme one.

According to the moderate thesis, a shared morality is the cement of society; without it there would be aggregates of individuals but no society. "A recognized morality" is, in Lord Devlin's words, "as necessary to society's existence as a recognized government,"[12] and though a particular act of immorality may not harm or endanger or corrupt others nor, when done in private, either shock or give offense to others, this does not conclude the matter. For we must not view conduct in isolation from its effect on the moral code: if we remember this, we can see that one who is "no menace to others" nonetheless may by his immoral conduct "threaten one of the great moral principles on which society is based."[13] In this sense the breach of moral principle is an offense "against society as a whole,"[14] and society may use the law to preserve its morality as it uses it to safeguard anything else essential to its existence. This is why "the suppression of vice is as much the law's business as the suppression of subversive activities."[15]

By contrast, the extreme thesis does not look upon a shared morality as of merely instrumental value analogous to ordered government, and it does not justify the punishment of immorality as a step taken, like the punishment of treason, to preserve society from dissolution or collapse. Instead, the enforcement of morality is regarded as a thing of value, even if immoral acts harm no one directly, or indirectly by weakening the moral cement of society. I do not say that it is possible to allot to one or other of these two theses every argument used, but they do, I think, characterize the main critical positions at the root of most arguments, and they incidentally exhibit an ambiguity in the expression "enforcing morality as such." Perhaps the clearest way of distinguishing the two theses is to see that there are always two levels at which we may ask whether some breach of positive morality is harmful. We may ask first, Does this act harm anyone independently of its repercussion on the shared morality of society? And second we may ask, Does this act affect the shared morality and thereby weaken society? The moderate thesis requires, if the punishment of the act is to be justified, an affirmative answer at least at the second level. The extreme thesis does not require an affirmative answer at either level.

Lord Devlin appears to defend the moderate thesis. I say "appears" because, though he says that society has the right to enforce a morality as such on the ground that a shared morality is essential to society's existence, it is not at all clear that for him the statement that immorality jeopardizes or weakens society is a statement of empirical fact. It seems sometimes to be an a priori assumption, and sometimes a necessary truth and a very odd one. The most important indication that this is so is that, apart from one vague reference to "history" showing that "the loosening of moral bonds is often the first stage of disintegration,"[16] no evidence is produced to show that deviation from accepted sexual morality, even by adults in private, is something which, like treason, threatens the existence of society. No reputable historian has maintained this thesis, and there is indeed much evidence against it. As a proposition of fact it is entitled to no more respect than the Emperor Justinian's statement that homosexuality was the cause of earthquakes.[17] Lord Devlin's belief in it, and his apparent indifference to the question of evidence, are at points traceable to an undiscussed assumption. This is that all morality—sexual morality together with the morality that forbids acts injurious to others such as killing, stealing, and dishonesty—forms a single seamless web, so that those who deviate from any part are likely or perhaps bound to deviate from the whole. It is of course clear (and one of the oldest insights of political theory) that society could not exist without a morality which mirrored and supplemented the law's proscription of conduct injurious to others. But there is again no evidence to support, and much to refute, the theory that those who deviate from conventional sexual morality are in other ways hostile to society.

There seems, however, to be central to Lord Devlin's thought something more interesting, though no more convincing, than the conception of social morality as a seamless web. For he appears to move from the acceptable proposition that *some* shared morality is essential to the existence of any society to the unacceptable proposition that a society is identical[18] with its morality as that is at any given moment of its history, so that a change in its morality is tantamount to the destruction of a society. The former proposition might be even accepted as a necessary rather than an empirical truth depending on a quite plausible definition of society as a body of men who hold certain moral views in common. But the latter proposition is absurd. Taken strictly, it would prevent us saying that the morality of a given society had changed, and would compel us instead to say that one society had disappeared and another one taken its place. But it is only on this absurd criterion of what it is for the same society to continue to exist that it could be asserted without evidence that any deviation from a society's shared morality threatens its existence.

It is clear that only this tacit identification of a society with its shared morality supports Lord Devlin's denial that there could be such a thing as private immorality and his comparison of sexual immorality, even when it takes place "in private," with treason. No doubt it is true that if deviations from conventional sexual morality are tolerated by the law and come to be known, the conventional morality might change in a permissive direction, though this does not seem to be the case with homosexuality in those European countries where it is not punishable by law. But even if the conventional morality did so change, the society in question would not have been destroyed or "subverted." We should compare such a development not to the violent overthrow of government but to a peaceful constitutional change in its form, consistent not only with the preservation of a society but with its advance.

Varieties of Enforcement

In the last lecture I distinguished a moderate and an extreme form of the thesis that the criminal law might justifiably be used to enforce morality. According to the moderate thesis, there is certainly a contrast between crimes obviously harmful to others (such as murder or assault) and mere immoral conduct, forbidden by law, which takes place between consenting adults in private. This contrast seems at first sight to warrant our regarding the legal prohibition and punishment of the latter as the enforcement of morality "as such." Nonetheless, according to this theory, once we grasp the truth that a society's morality is necessary for its very existence, it becomes clear that any immoral act, however private its performance, must in the long run be harmful because "it threatens the moral principles on which society is based" and so jeopardizes society's existence. So on this view the enforcement of morality (which is assumed to be required for its preservation) is necessary for the very existence of society and is justified for that reason.

The extreme thesis has many variants, and it is not always clear which of them its advocates are concerned to urge. According to some variants, the legal enforcement of morality is only of instrumental value: it is merely a means, though an indispensable one, for preserving morality, whereas the preservation of morality is the end, valuable in itself, which justifies its legal enforcement. According to other variants, there is something intrinsically valuable in the legal enforcement of morality. What is common to all varieties of the extreme thesis is that, unlike the moderate thesis, they do not hold the enforcement of morality or its preservation to be valuable merely because of their beneficial consequences in securing the existence of society.

It is to be observed that Lord Devlin hovers somewhat ambiguously between one form of the extreme thesis and the moderate thesis. For if we interpret his crucial statement that the preservation of a society's morality is necessary for its existence as a statement of fact (as the analogy with the suppression of treason suggests we should), then the continued existence of society is something distinguishable from the preservation of its morality. It is, in fact, a desirable consequence of the preservation of its morality, and, on the assumption that the enforcement of morality is identical with or required for its preservation, this desirable consequence justifies the enforcement of morality. So interpreted, Lord Devlin is an advocate of the moderate thesis and his argument is a utilitarian one. The objection to it is that his crucial statement of fact is unsupported by evidence; it is Utilitarianism without benefit of facts. If, on the other hand, we interpret his statement that any immorality, even in private, threatens the existence of society, not as an empirical statement but as a necessary truth (as the absence of evidence suggests we should), then the continued existence of a society is not something different from the preservation of its morality; it is identical with it. On this view the enforcement of morality is not justified by its valuable consequences in securing society from dissolution or decay. It is justified simply as identical with or required for the preservation of the society's morality. This is a form of the extreme thesis, disguised only by the tacit identification of a society with its morality which I criticized in the last lecture. . . .

The Preservation of Morality and Moral Conservatism

This last consideration brings us to what is really the central issue in the extreme thesis. Let us suppose, contrary to much evidence, that Stephen's picture of society and its moral mechanisms is a realistic one: that there really is a moral code in sexual matters supported by an overwhelming majority and that they are deeply disturbed when it is infringed even by adults in private; that the punishment of offenders really does sustain the sense that the conduct is immoral and without their punishment the prevalent morality would change in a permissive direction. The central question is: Can anything or nothing be said to support the claim that the prevention of this change and the maintenance of the moral status quo in a society's morality are values sufficient to offset the cost in human misery which legal enforcement entails? Is it simply a blank assertion, or does it rest on any critical principles connecting what is said to be of value here with other things of value?

Here certain discriminations are needed. There are three propositions concerning the value of preserving social morality which are in perennial danger of confusion. The first of these propositions is the truth that since all social moralities, whatever else they may contain, make provision in some degree for such universal values as individual freedom, safety of life, and protection from deliberately inflicted harm, there will always be much in social morality which is worth preserving even at the cost in terms of these same values which legal enforcement involves. It is perhaps misleading to say with Lord Devlin that social morality, so far as it secures these things, is of value because they are required for the preservation of society (on the contrary, the preservation of any particular society is of value because among other things it secures for human beings some measure of these universal values). It is indeed arguable that a human society in which these values are not recognized at all in its morality is neither an empirical nor a logical possibility, and that even if it were, such a society could be of no practical value for human beings. In conceding this much, however, we must beware of following Lord Devlin in thinking of social morality as a seamless web and of all its provisions as necessary for the existence of the society whose morality it is. We should with Mill be alive to the truth that though these essential universal values must be secured, society can not only survive individual divergences in other fields from its prevalent morality, but profit from them.

Second, there is the truth, less familiar and less easy to state in precise terms, that the spirit or attitude of mind which characterizes the practice of a social morality is something of very great value and indeed quite vital for men to foster and preserve in any society. For in the practice of any social morality there are necessarily involved what may be called *formal* values as distinct from the *material* values of its particular rules or content. In moral relationships with others, the individual sees questions of conduct from an impersonal point of view and applies general rules impartially to himself and to others; he is made aware of and takes account of the wants, expectations, and reactions of others, he exerts self-discipline and control in adapting his conduct to a system of reciprocal claims. These are universal virtues and indeed constitute the specifically moral attitude to conduct. It is true that these virtues are learnt in conforming to the morality of some particular society, but their value is not derived from the fact that they are there accounted virtues. We have only to conduct the Hobbesian experiment of imagining these virtues totally absent to see that they are vital for the conduct of any cooperative form of human life and any successful personal life. No principles of critical morality which paid the least attention to the most elementary facts of human nature and the conditions in which human life has to be led could propose to dispense with them. Hence if by the preservation of morality is meant the preservation of the moral attitude to conduct and its formal values, it is certainly true that it is a value. But, though true, this is really irrelevant to the issue before us; for the preservation of morality in this sense is not identical with and does not require the preservation from change of a society's moral code as it is at any given moment of that society's existence; and a fortiori it does not require the legal enforcement of its rules. The moral attitude to conduct has often survived the criticism, the infringement, and the ultimate relaxation of specific moral institutions. The use of legal punishment to freeze into immobility the morality dominant at a particular time in a society's existence may possibly succeed, but even where it does it contributes nothing to the survival of the animating spirit and formal values of social morality and may do much to harm them.

From the preservation of morality in this sense which is so clearly a value we must, then, distinguish mere moral conservatism. This latter amounts to the proposition that the preservation from change of any existent rule of a social morality, whatever its content, is a value and justifies its legal enforcement. This proposition would be at least intelligible if we could ascribe to all social morality the status which theological systems or the doctrine of the Law of Nature ascribes to some fundamental principles. Then, at least, some general principle would have been adduced to support the claim that preservation of any rule of social morality was a value justifying its legal enforcement; something would have been said to indicate the source of this asserted value. The application of these general principles to the case in hand would then be something to be discussed and argued, and moral conservatism would then be a form of critical morality to be used in the criticism of social institutions. It would not then be—as it is when dissociated from all such general principles—a brute dogma, asserting that the preservation of any social morality necessarily outweighs its cost in human misery and deprivation of freedom. In this dogmatic form it in effect withdraws positive morality from the scope of any moral criticism. . . .

This distinction between the use of coercion to enforce morality and other methods which we in fact use to preserve it, such as argument, advice, and exhortation, is both very important and much neglected in discussions of the present topic. . . .

Discussion, advice, argument—all these, since they leave the individual "the final judge," may according to Mill be used in a society where freedom is properly respected. We may even "obtrude" on another "considerations to aid his judgment and exhortations to strengthen his will."[19] We may in extreme cases "warn" him of our adverse judgment or feelings of distaste and contempt. We may avoid his company and caution others against it. Many might think that Mill here comes perilously near to sanctioning coercion even though he regards these things as "strictly inseparable from the unfavourable judgments of others"[20] and never to be inflicted for the sake of punishment. But if he erred in that direction, it is certainly clear that he recognized the important truth that in morality we are not forced to choose between deliberate coercion and indifference.

Moral Populism and Democracy

Mill's essay *On Liberty,* like Tocqueville's book *Democracy in America,* was a powerful plea for a clearheaded appreciation of the dangers that accompany the benefits of democratic rule. The greatest of the dangers, in their view, was not that in fact the majority might use their power to oppress a minority, but that, with the spread of democratic ideas, it might come to be thought unobjectionable that they should do so. For Mill, these dangers were part of the price to be paid for all that is so valuable in democratic government. He thought the price certainly worth paying; but he was much concerned to remind the supporters of democracy of the danger and the need for vigilance. "The limitation of the power of government over individuals loses none of its importance when the holders of power are regularly accountable to the community—that is to the strongest party therein."[21] . . .

It seems fatally easy to believe that loyalty to democratic principles entails acceptance of what may be termed moral populism: the view that the majority have a moral right to dictate how all should live. This is a misunderstanding of democracy which still menaces individual liberty, and I shall devote the remainder of this lecture to identifying the confusion on which it rests.[22]

The central mistake is a failure to distinguish the acceptable principle that political power is best entrusted to the majority from the unacceptable claim that what the majority do with that power is beyond criticism and must never be resisted. No one can be a democrat who does not accept the first of these, but no democrat need accept the second. Mill and many others have combined a belief in the democracy as the best—or least harmful—form of rule with the passionate conviction that there are many things which not even a democratic government may do. This combination of attitudes makes good sense, because, though a democrat is committed to the belief that democracy is better than other forms of government, he is not committed to the belief that it is perfect or infallible or never to be resisted. To support this last conclusion we need a further premise, going far beyond the simple assertion that it is better to entrust political power to the majority than to a selected class. This further premise must be some variant, secular or otherwise, of the identification of vox populi with vox Dei. One variant, which has been frequently referred to in these lectures, is the view that positive morality supported by an overwhelming moral majority is immune from criticism.

It is not, of course, surprising that these confusions have been made or that they survive even in democracies like the United States, where the rights of individuals are protected to some extent from majorities by a written constitution; or in England, where for long the elected member of Parliament has been considered to be the representative but not the delegate of his constituents. For there are in the actual working of democracy many forces likely to encourage the belief that the principle of democratic rule *means* that the majority are always right. Even the most high-minded politician may want to stay in office, and a pliant or passive attitude to what the majority thinks right makes this easier than a stern adherence to the theory that his duty is to do what he thinks right, and then to accept his dismissal if he cannot persuade the majority to retain him. But what is understandable as a temptation to elected legislators may yet be regretted in those not under a similar temptation. Whatever other arguments there may be for the enforcement of morality, no one should think even when popular morality is supported by an "overwhelming majority" or marked by widespread "intolerance, indignation, and disgust" that loyalty to democratic principles requires him to admit that its imposition on a minority is justified.

Conclusion
I hope that these three lectures are clear enough and short enough to make a detailed summary unnecessary. Instead I shall say a word in conclusion about the method of argument which I have followed. I have from the beginning assumed that anyone who raises, or is willing

to debate, the question whether it is justifiable to enforce morality, accepts the view that the actual institutions of any society, including its positive morality, are open to criticism. Hence the proposition that it is justifiable to enforce morality is, like its negation, a thesis of critical morality requiring for its support some general critical principle. It cannot be established or refuted simply by pointing to the actual practices or morality of a particular society or societies. Lord Devlin, whose thesis I termed the moderate thesis, seems to accept this position, but I have argued that the general critical principle which he deploys, namely, that a society has the right to take any step necessary for its preservation, is inadequate for his purpose. There is no evidence that the preservation of a society requires the enforcement of its morality "as such." His position only appears to escape this criticism by a confused definition of what a society is.

I have also assumed from the beginning that anyone who regards this question as open to discussion necessarily accepts the critical principle, central to all morality, that human misery and the restriction of freedom are evils; for that is why the legal enforcement of morality calls for justification. I then endeavored to extricate, and to free from ambiguity of statement, the general principles underlying several varieties of the more extreme thesis that the enforcement of morality or its preservation from change were valuable apart from their beneficial consequences in preserving society. These principles in fact invite us to consider as values, for the sake of which we should restrict human freedom and inflict the misery of punishment on human beings, things which seem to belong to the pre-history of morality and to be quite hostile to its general spirit. They include mere outward conformity to moral rules induced simply by fear; the gratification of feelings of hatred for the wrongdoer or his "retributory" punishment, even where there has been no victim to be avenged or to call for justice; the infliction of punishment as a symbol or expression of moral condemnation; the mere insulation from change of any social morality however repressive or barbarous. No doubt I have not *proved* these things not to be values worth their price in human suffering and loss of freedom; it may be enough to have shown what it is that is offered for the price.

NOTES

1. John Stuart Mill, *On Liberty*, chapter 1.
2. Ibid.

3. James Fitzjames Stephen, *Liberty, Equality, Fraternity* (2d ed.; London: Smith Elgard & Co., 1874).

4. Ibid., 162.

5. The Hon. Sir Patrick Devlin, *The Enforcement of Morals* (London: Oxford University Press, 1959).

6. Devlin, *The Enforcement of Morals*, 8.

7. Ibid.

8. Ibid., 9.

9. Mill, *On Liberty*, chapter 1.

10. Devlin, *The Enforcement of Morals*, 8.

11. See, for other possible explanations of these rules, Graham Hughes, "Morals and the Criminal Law," *Yale Law Journal* (1961) 622.

12. Devlin, *The Enforcement of Morals*, 13.

13. Ibid., 8.

14. Ibid.

15. Ibid., 15.

16. Ibid., 14–15.

17. Justinian *Novels*, 77 Cap. 1 and 141.

18. See, for this important point, Richard Wollheim, "Crime, Sin, and Mr. Justice Devlin," *Encounter* (November 1959) 34.

19. Mill, *On Liberty*, chap. 4.

20. Ibid.

21. Ibid., chapter 1.

22. There are vestiges of this confusion in Lord Devlin's latest contribution to the present topic ("Law, Democracy, and Morality," *University of Pennsylvania Law Review* 110 [1962] 635–49). For he there (p. 639) asserts that "in a democracy a legislator will assume that the morals of his society are good and true; if he does not he should not be playing an active part in government. . . . But he has not to vouch for their goodness and truth. His mandate is to preserve the essentials of his society, not to reconstruct them according to his own ideas." But elsewhere (p. 644) he concedes that a legislator "has a very wide discretion in determining how far he will go in the direction of the law as he thinks it ought to be." Lord Devlin's main concern in this essay is to establish against "the view of the philosophers" (*sic*) that there is no objection to morality being a matter for the popular vote (p. 642), that morality is a question of fact (p. 649), and that in a democracy "educated men cannot be put in a separate category for the decision of moral questions" (p. 643). But as far as positive morality is concerned, few would dispute these contentions. The question remains, What justifies its enforcement by law? As to that, Lord Devlin seems content with his previous arguments and his analogy with treason, criticized above.

3

*Religion and the Legislation of Morals**

Frederick S. Carney

Eleven years ago in England the Wolfenden Committee issued its report recommending that homosexuality between consenting adults in private cease to be punishable by criminal law.[1] During the same year in America the Supreme Court decided in the Roth case that literature judged to be obscene under a "prurient interest" test is not protected by the First Amendment, and therefore its public distribution may be restricted by criminal statute.[2] Both the Wolfenden Report and the Roth case aroused vigorous popular feelings for and against the positions they affirmed. They also elicited from some of England's and America's finest jurists and scholars an illuminating controversy over the broader question of the legislation of morals. Essentially that question is, What condition (or conditions) should be satisfied to justify a society's imposition of legal punishment for violations of its social morality? Presumably the answer to this question will help us to determine what employment of criminal law (if any) should be made for acts not only of homosexuality and obscenity, but also of adultery, polygamy, incest, abortion, drunkenness, gambling, cruelty to animals, theft, usury, falsehood, assault, and murder.

Two main types of answers have been provided by the participants in this controversy. According to one type, it is sufficient that the act be clearly and strongly condemned by the positive morality of the

---

*First published in *Soundings* 51 (1968) 432–47.

society, whatever that morality may be, for it to be eligible for punishment by criminal law. It is not necessary, although it is often the case, that such an act be injurious to others. Practical considerations may mediate against legislating punishment for such an act, but in principle society is entitled to do so. What justifies such entitlement? It has sometimes been suggested that the justification is simply that society has a right to punish legally what it condemns morally. It has also been proposed that the justification derives from the need of society to protect its existence, coupled with the assumption that violations of its positive morality may threaten that existence. Or again, justification may be attempted on the ground of a society's concern to defend its moral code (or moral institutions) from changes it opposes.

Lord Devlin, perhaps the foremost advocate of this type of answer, would seem to assign some role to each of these justifications. He writes that "there is only one explanation of what has hitherto been accepted as the basis of the criminal law and that is that there are certain standards of behavior or moral principles which society requires to be observed."[3] He has also suggested that "an established morality is as necessary as good government to the welfare of society. . . . History shows that the loosening of moral bonds is often the first stage of disintegration, so that society is justified in taking the same steps to preserve its moral code as it does to preserve its government and other essential institutions."[4] And he has invited us to inquire whether, looking at some act such as homosexuality "calmly and dispassionately, we regard it as a vice so abominable that its mere presence is an offence. If that is the genuine feeling of the society in which we live, I do not see how society can be denied the right to eradicate it."[5]

The other main type of answer denies that popular moral disapproval, however vigorous, should be sufficient to make an act eligible for legislation imposing criminal sanctions. It affirms the necessity of believing upon reasonable grounds that appreciable harm results from the performance of the act. Indeed, the harm should be of such an extent as to warrant the infliction of misery and the deprivation of liberty that punishment and the threat thereof entail. Supporters of this position point out that the coercions of criminal law affect not only offenders, but also non-offenders for whom the threat of punishment may lead to restrictions upon freedom and the suppression, often painful, of desires. They hold that the avoidance of misery and the exercise of liberty are human values of very great importance, and that interference with them is an evil that is to be justified only in terms of these values themselves. They therefore appeal beyond positive morality to critical morality, and propose the employment of a harm test, which would authorize legal punishment only to prevent other appreciable injury, as the justifying criterion for the legislation of morality.

H. L. A. Hart, who has perhaps best represented this position in the recent controversy, writes that "the use of legal coercion by any society calls for justification as something prima facie objectionable to be tolerated only for the sake of some countervailing good."[6] Although he thinks that "there may be grounds justifying the legal coercion of the individual other than the prevention of harm to others"[7] what he apparently has in mind are extensions of the notion of injury beyond what some persons might narrowly construe as "harm to others." Chief among these grounds are the preservation of society (but not the preservation from change of a society's conventional morals as such), paternalism ("the protection of people against themselves" in such matters as the sale of narcotics), discouragement of public indecency (by prohibiting, for example, sexual acts in public to the extent that they constitute unreasonable shock or offense to the sensitivities of others), and the prevention of cruelty to animals (on the basis that animals, like human beings, suffer).[8]

Now it is a fact that religious men and women are to be found on both sides of this controversy. Indeed, they have been taking sides on it long before it received its present sharpened focus at the hands of contemporary jurists and scholars. Moreover, they are often influenced in their positions by grounds that are explicitly or implicitly religious. Even though we live in a secular age, religious beliefs and motivations continue to play a major role in the way in which many people look at and respond to public questions such as this one.

This is a different point from one made by both Devlin and Hart. Both acknowledge an historic connection of religion with morality and law. Devlin inquires where the law gets its authority to enforce morals and how it determines what morals to enforce. "Undoubtedly as a matter of history," he writes, "it derived both from Christian teaching. But I think that the strict logician is right when he says that the law can no longer rely on doctrines in which citizens are entitled to disbelieve."[9] Hart observes that "no doubt a critical morality based on the theory that all social morality had the status of divine commands or of eternal truths discovered by reason would not for obvious reasons now seem plausible."[10] What is of interest in this essay, however, is not this historic connection that earlier prevailed, a connection in which the appeal to religion in matters of morality and law once had, but no longer has, official authority for all persons. Rather our interest is in a contemporary phenomenon, one in which the influence of religion in deciding matters of morality and law continues to be accepted by some, but not all, persons.

It has sometimes been suggested that this influence is highly improper.[11] Of course, if what is involved is an attempt to enforce religious beliefs, and practices expressing them, on those who are not persuaded by them, as is sometimes done for example in the maintenance of public school prayers, the point is well taken. For this violates the conscience of those who do not share these beliefs. Or if recourse is had to religious beliefs of a simply dogmatic and irrational sort by a citizen or a legislator in the exercise of his suffrage, as for example in support of or opposition to alcohol or birth control legislation, we should have to agree that this is indeed improper. For this makes inaccessible to reasoned public discussion the grounds of one's moral and legal judgment. But what we have in mind is something else. It is the employment by a person of his full and reasoned understanding of the depth and dimensions of human life in the exercise of his judgment on public issues, some of which understanding may be an integral part of a religious view of life. Surely what a person thinks about the nature and destiny of man is often going to influence not only his private but also his public life. And it would seem highly undesirable, if not impossible, to try to root this out of his participation in public life.

Something of this sort is what Basil Mitchell has argued in a recent and important book on the legislation of morals. He has objected, rightly I believe, to the notion that "religious considerations, as they affect morality, should have no place in law making."[12] And he has done so because he holds that persons who are persuaded by a religious view of life may find therein illumination of "the human condition" that informs their understanding of morality and law and that shapes in part their contribution to public life. Mitchell calls attention to a statement by S. I. Benn and R. S. Peters that "democracy presupposes a readiness to consult all experience, to respect all persons as sources of claims and arguments," and observes that if this is so then democracy "cannot refuse in principle to listen to any who have a serious case to state and who accept the conventions of a free society."[13]

Nevertheless, I think Mitchell has misunderstood the appropriate relation of religion to morality and law, and that this misunderstanding has wrongly led him to propose an answer to our basic question about the legislation of morality that falls largely within the Devlin type of position. I suggest, to the contrary, that a more adequate understanding of the relation of religion to morality and law should lead religious men to lend support to an answer closer to the Hart type of position. The development of these two notions will be the task of the remainder of this essay.

Mitchell's position would seem to have four basic elements to it, which I shall first reconstruct from a variety of statements throughout his book and then criticize. My criticism will be intended to apply not only to Mitchell and to those who share his particular theological beliefs (in this instance a determinate set of Christian affirmations), but also to anyone who develops his argument in the form that Mitchell does even though his theological beliefs may be somewhat different.

(1) It is affirmed that every person is a child of God, made in his image, redeemed in Jesus Christ, and destined for eternal life. To make this affirmation is also to make love the supreme principle of moral action. Although it is not always clear what love specifically requires, in general it can be said that it demands that we be responsive to the good of each person.[14]

(2) It is nevertheless clear that there are specific Christian moral ideals in at least two main areas. The first pertains to questions of life and death, especially to abortion and euthanasia. Abortion is, either to be condemned altogether or else to be kept under such strict control that it is not to be countenanced, for example, on the sole ground that a defective child is likely to be born. Euthanasia also is prohibited by Christian moral ideals, even if a person dying slowly and agonizingly requests it. The other area pertains to sex and marriage. Outside of a life-long mutual commitment of one man and one woman the use of the sexual organs is condemned by Christian ideals. Thus monogamy is required, polygamy prohibited, and acts of fornication, adultery, and homosexuality condemned.[15]

(3) Essential to the existence of every society is a shared morality. Part of this shared morality is composed of those universal values for which, as Hart has said, all societies must to some degree make provision if they are to be viable, such as individual liberty and protection from deliberately inflicted harm. But another part is composed of "essential institutions" whose precise form may vary

from one society to another, and which are usually determined by the ideals of a particular society. In England and America monogamy is among these essential institutions. (Our form of property is another, but we shall not consider it here.) Now monogamy got into our shared morality because it is Christian but, as Devlin writes, "it remains there because it is built into the house in which we live and could not be removed without bringing it down." These considerations being so, it is meaningful to speak of harm to individuals not only directly but also indirectly through a weakening of their essential institutions. At the same time, the protection of such institutions, and thus the protection of individuals from harm, can be enhanced by maintaining an ethos (or moral atmosphere) that supports them and by reinforcing acceptable moral behavior through sanctions against offenders.[16]

(4) The function of law is not only to protect individuals from harm but also "to protect the essential institutions of a society." In so doing, law may in principle also be employed to maintain the society's ethos from corruption and to reinforce moral behavior by imposing criminal punishments on offenders. However, practical considerations (such as the difficulty or inequity of enforcement) may be of sufficient import to weight the balance against employing legal sanctions in some types of cases in which the society is entitled to do so in principle. Perhaps homosexuality between consenting adults in private falls in this category.[17]

These are the main elements of Mitchell's position as I understand them. Taken together they indicate one way by which religious men move from theological affirmation to the legislation of morals. Although there are a number of challenges that could be made to this position, I shall limit my criticism to three rather fundamental points.

The first is Mitchell's characterization of Christian morality. I can perhaps best get at this by asking why in (2) any sexual act outside of monogamous marriage is to be judged wrong. The answer Mitchell seems to be giving is that such an act would violate a traditional Christian ideal. Historically Christians have affirmed a monogamous norm, and for the most part they do so today. It is simply part of the Christian way of life, as polygamy might be part of the way of life for some other religious group. Now to make this kind of claim is to appeal simply to positive morality, albeit in this instance a religious positive morality. It leaves still to be determined whether this is what the positive morality ought to be. A given society may maintain the practice of segregation as part of its positive morality, but the practice itself needs moral justification. An adequate morality requires a critical or trans-positive dimension, a way of morally evaluating and justifying the positive norms it affirms. Otherwise it is left defenseless against the question, "I agree that this is the moral practice of your group, but is it *really* moral?"[18]

Perhaps Mitchell finds a critical dimension of Christian morality in the theological affirmations indicated in (1). To do so would not only identify love as the critical principle, but also inform our understanding of this principle, and of its demand for responsiveness to the good of each person, by exemplifying it in the cross of Christ and the redemptive concern of God for all men presumably revealed therein. This would be in keeping with Mitchell's earlier suggestion that a religious view of life may illumine our understanding of human nature and moral action. To think of Christian morality in this way, however, is to make the validity of the norms of Christian positive morality dependent upon critical justification by the principle of Christian love. Thus traditional ideals, such as that sexual intercourse is to be restricted to monogamous marriage, would have to be considered in principle defeasible. And there is good reason to doubt that Mitchell is willing that they should be so considered. Although he is prepared to outline possible utilitarian support for Christian ideals to persuade secularists that such ideals are not irrational, he does not attempt to justify them by means of a Christian critical morality. He merely asserts them as basic religious concepts. Note his explanation of the traditional view of sexual intercourse. "To the Christian it has, in fact, a sacramental character as the appropriate expression of a life-long union. And it is here that specifically religious concepts make their entry. Marriage is thought of as ordained for the procreation of children and the mutual comfort and consolation the one ought to have of the other, and the sexual organs are thought of as designed for this purpose. Hence use of them outside marriage is to be condemned."[19] Apparently monogamous marriage is the moral ideal for Christians not because it is critically justified by Christian love and its demand for responsiveness to the good of men, but simply because it has traditionally been thought of by Christians as the moral ideal.

It may be, however, that I have misunderstood Mitchell, and that he does hold Christian positive moral ideals to be in principle defeasible. There is one passage in his book that lends support to this alternative construction of his view. "If factual investigation can be appealed to in support of theological insights—if the proven evils of broken homes can be adduced in support of the divinely ordained harmony of marriage—then, were this support to be lacking or were evidence to the contrary to accumulate, the theological position would to that extent be weakened and might, in principle, even be refuted."[20] But this leaves open the question of the extent to which factual investigation is to be considered relevant to the determination of the validity of a particular ideal. In another passage on questions of life and death, Mitchell writes of "the Christian's unwillingness to give overriding importance to the prevention or relief of pain. Where for many secular humanists the claims of compassion point unambiguously to the cessation of a painful situation, the Christian sees life also as a task to be performed where some good can be achieved, even if it be only that of dutiful obedience."[21] Apparently dutiful obedience to an ideal is to be upheld in this instance whether or not the ideal can be justified by looking at the results of the factual investigation of suffering in relation to the critical principle of Christian love. Thus, even if Mitchell is in principle willing to accept the defeasibility of traditional Christian ideals, he seems in fact to be quite reluctant to do so.

What then does Mitchell mean by Christian morality? It would seem that he understands it to be a series of rather specific norms or ideals (pertaining to fornication, adultery, homosexuality, euthanasia, abortion, and such matters) taken together with some basic theological affirmations of Christian thought. However, in light of the rapid medical and social changes of our society these norms may or may not now be appropriate expressions of the theological affirmations with which they are identified or of some central critical feature thereof such as Christian love. We are therefore justified in inquiring whether all the norms or ideals Mitchell identifies with Christian morality are truly moral. Some of them may turn out to be elements of a social conservatism got up to look like moral requirements of the Christian religion.

The second point concerns Mitchell's understanding in (3) of "essential institutions" within the shared morality of a society, and of their relation to specific norms and ideals of moral behavior. Take the example of monogamy, which Mitchell considers to be one of these institutions. In what sense is monogamy essential to our society? Surely not in the sense that no society can exist without it. Some societies exist that organize their marital relations along polygamous lines. Monogamy is not therefore a universal value as such. With this

Mitchell agrees.[22] Rather it is in the sense, according to Mitchell, that monogamy has long been a characteristic part of our society and is integrally built into it. To change away from it now would alter not only our marital relations, but also other institutions such as property and education.

It is to be noted, however, that Mitchell does not indicate how we are to justify monogamy in preference to polygamy other than to observe that it is an integral part of "the house in which we live." This is tantamount to saying that it is essential because it exists in our society. If polygamy were the actual form by which we organize our marital relations, would it, rather than monogamy, be essential to our society?

Mitchell might argue for monogamy on the basis that it is less harmful in a technological society than any other familial form, or that it is more beneficial, or that it is justified by some other critical principle. He does not do so, however, except to observe that institutions which tend flagrantly to violate universal values (such as a sexual system based on rape apparently would) are to be condemned and understood to fall outside the range of what could properly be meant by essential institutions. We are therefore left with that conclusion that an essential institution is merely one that happens (extreme cases aside) to be a major part of our positive morality.

This being so, it does not follow that the failure to protect such an institution would necessarily result in harm to the persons who live within it. For Mitchell has not established that the loss or alteration of an essential institution, as he has characterized it, is harm-producing. He has established only that it would result in a significant change in the positive morality of the society. Although it may be true that the "protection of individuals from harm is not a purpose which can be realized independently of the protection of the institutions under which they live,"[23] it is not true that all the institutions under which they live need to be protected in order to protect individuals from harm. The pity is that Mitchell's category of essential institutions does not help us to determine which institutions need protection for this reason.

Even if we assume that monogamy is such an institution, the problem remains of determining what specific norms and ideals are implied by monogamy. Are all sexual acts outside a life-long union between one man and one woman to be proscribed? Or are some sexual acts outside such a union such that they do not threaten the existence of the institution and therefore should be morally permitted under specified conditions? It must be apparent that there are different assessments of what about monogamy is so important that its protection by society is sought, and that these assessments give rise to different views concerning what specific norms and ideals are appropriate in such matters as fornication, adultery, divorce, and homosexuality. Here again we require recourse to critical moral thought that transcends positive morality to help us to arrive at reasonable answers to this problem. Without such recourse we are in danger of merely reiterating the moral conventions of our society or religious group, which conventions, even if religious in origin, may or may not be truly moral.

For the third point, I shall comment briefly on Mitchell's position on the legislation of morals (4), and on his understanding of the role of religion therein. He is apparently willing to employ penal sanctions to protect a society's essential institutions, to preserve its ethos from corruption, and to reinforce (within discernible limits) its moral code.[24] His willingness to do so would seem to rest prima facie on a harm test. For he believes that harm to the essential institutions, to the ethos, or to the moral code of a society will in turn bring harm to individuals. But this connection is not necessarily true, as I have already pointed out regarding essential institutions. Some "harms" to an institution, ethos, or code may actually reduce harm or increase benefit to individuals by freeing them from oppression or unreasonable burdens. Believing as he does, however, Mitchell (like Devlin) is willing to legislate the positive morality as such of a society upon its members. And thus his basic test does not (as with Hart) center on actual harm to persons either directly or indirectly. Rather it hinges on the determination of whether some norm or ideal is an actual part of the society's positive morality. If it is, it is eligible for penal legislation to enforce it, even though practical considerations may weigh against actually legislating it in some instances.

Even though Mitchell has argued for the relevance of religious considerations to civil law, he does not employ religious categories overtly in the major summary of his position on the legislation of morals near the end of his book.[25] Instead he refers to essential institutions, ethos, and moral code. This, in itself, raises no insurmountable problem in relating religion to law, for he may merely have translated his understanding of Christian positive morality (2) into these more widely-accepted secular categories (3). Thus the Christian ideal of monogamous marriage can be expressed as an essential institution in the secular realm. What does give rise to a problem, however, is that

Mitchell's discussion of positive morality, both Christian and secular, seems to lack a critical dimension, and thus a basis for justifying ideals and institutions in positive morality as truly moral. This is all the more surprising in that among his central theological affirmations (1) is the critical principle of Christian love. Yet he seems not to apply this principle to positive morality and law either directly or indirectly through other categories. Perhaps this is because of a reluctance to make certain traditional ideals defeasible. Whatever the reasons, he is not only left with Devlin's type of answer to our basic question on the legislation of morality, an answer that cannot help us to determine what finally are the moral requirements in justifying morals legislation; he is also unable to point out the relevance and illuminating power of religious considerations, except possibly positive ones, in problems of morality and law.

I shall now outline an alternative position on the relation of religion to morality and law. It involves, among other things, the Hart type of answer to our basic question about the legislation of morality. Like Mitchell's position, it has four elements.

(1′) The same as Mitchell's (1). It will suit present purposes.

(2′) There are specific moral norms that collectively constitute a corpus of Christian positive morality. Although many of these norms have derived from a long and distinguished tradition, they are justified not by that tradition as such but by their transparency to what Christian love requires in the areas and under the circumstances to which they apply. Not all norms in the corpus of Christian positive morality are justifiable by this test. Among those that are justifiable, some express basic obligations in that their general acceptance is in the interests of all persons. Others express ultra obligations in that those who accept them are committed to the voluntary relinquishment of their own interests in some regard on behalf of pressing needs of others.[26] Authentic religious faith not only clarifies these obligations, but also by renewing its possessor's sense of identity with his world increases his motivation for more ready acceptance of these obligations. The notion that every person is a child of God in (1′) is one of the ways of articulating such faith.

(3′) Every society has a shared morality. Part of it is composed of the norms and obligations without which the society could not survive, such as at least minimum respect for the preservation of individual liberty and for the avoidance of deliberately inflicted injury. Another part pertains to norms and obligations imposed upon all and perhaps in the interests of all, but not strictly speaking necessary to the existence of the society. Still another part may be norms and obligations imposed upon all but which cannot be critically justified in terms of generalized human interests. Furthermore, the shared morality will experience change from time to time as the conditions change in which the interests of men are expressed. The concern of religious faith in shared morality is not in its unaltered preservation. Rather it is in its most lively representation of the true interests of men. The religious man, provided he is not superficially locked into one positive morality or other, should bring to developing changes in the shared morality a breadth of perception into the things that are in the true interests of men and the things that are injurious, as well as a depth of commitment on behalf of the neighbor to the service of those interests and the avoidance of those injuries.

(4′) Legislation to impose criminal sanctions is to be justified to the extent that, on balance, it prevents greater injury to human interests. Men of religion have no real stake in legislating positive morality as such, even under the guise of preventing harm to our moral institutions, ethos, or code. Aside from the fact that such legislation does not truly serve the interests of the neighbor, it also acts as a deliberate disservice to him by imposing morally unjustifiable punishments.

A number of observations could be made about this alternative to Mitchell's understanding of the relations of religion to morality and law. I shall limit myself, however, to three points. The first pertains to the general characterization of religious morality. The characterization I have applied to it combines a ready acknowledgment of an important role for specific norms of religious positive morality with an acceptance of their defeasibility in light of critical religious considerations. It avoids (or at least mitigates) a problem that often confronts religion in contemporary discussions of the legislation of morals. This is the representation of religious concern for morality as a largely uncritical defense of "morals" in such matters as fornication, gambling, and liquor. What in fact characterizes authentic religious morality most, if the major testimonies of Western faith are to be believed, is a profound concern for the avoidance of harm to human beings and for the protection and development of their interests. Its traditional norms of positive morality have been mostly derivative from this concern.

It should be noted that the testing of traditional norms of positive morality by critical considerations is not a new departure in religious morality. Reformation religion re-examined the longstanding rule on usury, and significantly modified it in light of basic moral principles when applied to the changing economic and social conditions of the times. Likewise, although contemporary religious bodies may be somewhat divided at the present time in their handling of the traditional moral prohibition against birth control, a large number of them have already reviewed their earlier positions to ascertain what obligations love can most appropriately require of modern men and women when they are confronted with a radically changed medical and social context of sexual intercourse. For the most part they have so modified their earlier positive norm that it now makes obligatory under certain conditions what had been forbidden. From these and other examples that could be offered, it would seem that this characterization of religious morality as involving the defeasibility of its positive norms has clear, if not uncontested, standing in Western man's religious experience.

My second point arises out of a distinction between the shared morality and the moral fabric of a society. The former, although it includes the entire range of moral obligations that, rightly or wrongly, are incumbent upon all persons in the society, is still only a very small part of the latter. For the moral fabric of a society also includes both the vast networks of obligations that are shared only within sub-groups of the society and the inestimable number of ultra obligations voluntarily assumed by various members of the society.

This being so, it is not at all clear that the legislation of shared morality, in order to maintain the ethos or moral atmosphere of a society, would be particularly effective in doing so. Large ranges of behavior relevant to the ethos would be uncovered thereby, not to speak of the increase in suffering that would be entailed by the imposition of punishment upon offenders against the shared morality and by the threat thereof upon non-offenders. On the other hand, it is open to members of the society to influence its ethos by voluntarily assuming ultra obligations toward those with pressing needs. To do so places the burden of contributing to the ethos upon the shoulders of those so opting rather than upon those who reluctantly happen to get caught in the net of the law. This recourse may be an especially appropriate one for religiously oriented men and women with a deep sense of personal calling to serve the needs of others.

The third and final point concerns the way in which churches and other religious organizations could most appropriately relate themselves to the legislation of morals. In the past, of course, they have often conducted their activity very much as pressure groups mobilizing their members on behalf of the legislation of particular norms of positive morality they approved, especially in matters of alcohol, birth control, obscenity, horseracing and gambling. I have been arguing, however, that the legislation of morals cannot be morally justified by appeal to positive morality alone, that it requires the discriminatory judgment of critical morality. Assuming this to be true, it follows that persons who participate in these decisions, in whatever capacity, ought to be prepared so far as possible to reflect critically on the justification for the legislation they are approving or disapproving. This is especially true of religious men who wish to bring the critical insights of religion to bear on public morality and law. It would therefore seem that the most appropriate manner for churches to be related to the legislation of morals is in the critical training of their members in problems of religion, morality, and law.

NOTES

1. *Report of the Committee on Homosexual Offenses and Prostitution,* (1957) Command Papers No. 274.

2. *Roth* v. *United States,* 354 U.S. 476 (1957). More precisely, the present test is that material is obscene if "(a) the dominant theme of the material taken as a whole appeals to a prurient interest in sex; (b) the material is patently offensive because it affronts contemporary standards relating to the description or representation of sexual matters; and (c) the material is utterly without redeeming social value." *Memoirs* v. *Massachusetts* (*Fanny Hill*), 383 U.S. 413 (1966).

3. The Hon. Sir Patrick Devlin, *The Enforcement of Morals* (London: Oxford University Press, 1965) 6–7. An earlier essay, "The Enforcement of Morals," *Proceedings of the British Academy* 45 (1959), is reprinted as the first chapter in this book. See also Eugene V. Rostow, "The Enforcement of Morals," in *The Sovereign Prerogative* (New Haven and London: Yale University Press, 1962) 45–80; and Norman St. John-Stevas, *Law and Morals* (New York: Hawthorn Books, 1964) esp. 23–31.

4. Devlin, *The Enforcement of Morals,* 13.

5. Ibid., 17.

6. H. L. A. Hart, *Law, Liberty, and Morality* (Stanford: Stanford University Press, 1963) 20. See also idem, "Immorality and Treason," in *The Law as Literature* (ed. L. J. Blom-Cooper [London: The Bodley Head, 1961]) 220–27; idem, "The Enforcement of Morality," in *The Morality of the Criminal Law* (Jerusalem: Magnes Press, 1965) 31–54; Graham Hughes, "Morals and the Criminal Law," *Yale Law Journal* 71 (1962) 662–83; and Ronald Dworkin, "Lord Devlin and the Enforcement of Morals," *Yale Law Journal* 75 (1966) 986–1005.

7. Hart, *Law, Liberty, and Morality,* 5.

8. Ibid., 18–19, 31–33, 34, 38–48.

9. Devlin, *The Enforcement of Morals*, 7.

10. Hart, *Law, Liberty, and Morality*, 73. See also p. 23.

11. See, e.g., Louis Henkin, "Morals and the Constitution: The Sin of Obscenity," *Columbia Law Review* 63 (1963) 391–414.

12. Basil Mitchell, *Law, Morality, and Religion in a Secular Society* (London: Oxford University Press, 1967) 100.

13. Ibid., 130–31. The Benn and Peters quotation is taken by Mitchell from their *Social Principles of the Democratic State* (London: George Allen & Unwin, 1959) 353.

14. Mitchell, *Law, Morality, and Religion*, 107–9, 117–18.

15. Ibid., 108–14.

16. Ibid., 18–35, 119–21, 131–33. See also Hart, *Law, Liberty, and Morality*, 70; Devlin, *The Enforcement of Morals*, 9.

17. Mitchell, *Law, Morality, and Religion*, 134–35. Devlin apparently has reached the same conclusion regarding homosexuality.

18. Ronald Dworkin's analysis of Devlin's understanding of morality employs the categories of "morality in an anthropological sense" and "morality in a discriminatory sense" in a manner very similar to my use of the terms positive and critical morality. Dworkin, "Lord Devlin," 994–1002. See also Hart, *Law, Liberty, and Morality*, 17–24.

19. Mitchell, *Law, Morality, and Religion*, 112.

20. Ibid., 118.

21. Ibid., 110.

22. Ibid., 120, 131–32.

23. Ibid., 68.

24. Ibid., 134–35.

25. Ibid.

26. See Russell Grice, *The Grounds of Moral Judgment* (Cambridge: Cambridge University Press, 1967).

PART TWO

THE INTERRELATION OF
LAW AND MORALITY

4

Positivism and the Separation of Law and Morals*

H. L. A. Hart

At the close of the eighteenth century and the beginning of the nineteenth the most earnest thinkers in England about legal and social problems and the architects of great reforms were the great Utilitarians. Two of them, Bentham and Austin, constantly insisted on the need to distinguish, firmly and with the maximum of clarity, law as it is from law as it ought to be. This theme haunts their work, and they condemned the natural-law thinkers precisely because they had blurred this apparently simple but vital distinction. . . .

There are therefore two dangers between which insistence on this distinction will help us to steer: the danger that law and its authority may be dissolved in man's conceptions of what law ought to be and the danger that the existing law may supplant morality as a final test of conduct and so escape criticism.

In view of later criticisms it is also important to distinguish several things that the Utilitarians did not mean by insisting on their separation of law and morals. They certainly accepted many of the things that might be called "the intersection of law and morals." First, they never denied that, as a matter of historical fact, the development of legal systems had been powerfully influenced by moral opinion, and, conversely, that moral standards had been profoundly influenced by law, so that the content of many legal rules mirrored moral rules or

*First published in *Harvard Law Review* 71 (1958) 593–629.

principles. It is not in fact always easy to trace this historical causal connection, but Bentham was certainly ready to admit its existence; so too Austin spoke of the "frequent coincidence"[1] of positive law and morality and attributed the confusion of what law is with what law ought to be to this very fact.

Second, neither Bentham nor his followers denied that by explicit legal provisions moral principles might at different points be brought into a legal system and form part of its rules, or that courts might be legally bound to decide in accordance with what they thought just or best. Bentham indeed recognized, as Austin did not, that even the supreme legislative power might be subjected to legal restraints by a constitution[2] and would not have denied that moral principles, like those of the fifth amendment, might form the content of such legal constitutional restraints. Austin differed in thinking that restraints on the supreme legislative power could not have the force of law, but would remain merely political or moral checks;[3] but of course he would have recognized that a statute, for example, might confer a delegated legislative power and restrict the area of its exercise by reference to moral principles.

What both Bentham and Austin were anxious to assert were the following two simple things: first, in the absence of an expressed constitutional or legal provision, it could not follow from the mere fact that a rule violated standards of morality that it was not a rule of law; and, conversely, it could not follow from the mere fact that a rule was morally desirable that it was a rule of law. . . .

The Utilitarians thought that the essence of a legal system could be conveyed if the notion of a command were supplemented by that of a habit of obedience. The simple scheme was this: What is a command? It is simply an expression by one person of the desire that another person should do or abstain from some action, accompanied by a threat of punishment which is likely to follow disobedience. Commands are laws if two conditions are satisfied: first, they must be general; second, they must be commanded by what (as both Bentham and Austin claimed) exists in every political society whatever its constitutional form, namely, a person or a group of persons who are in receipt of habitual obedience from most of the society but pay no such obedience to others. These persons are its sovereign. Thus law is the command of the uncommanded commanders of society—the creation of the legally untrammelled will of the sovereign who is by definition outside the law.

It is easy to see that this account of a legal system is threadbare.

One can also see why it might seem that its inadequacy is due to the omission of some essential connection with morality. The situation which the simple trilogy of command, sanction, and sovereign avails to describe, if you take these notions at all precisely, is like that of a gunman saying to his victim, "Give me your money or your life." The only difference is that in the case of a legal system the gunman says it to a large number of people who are accustomed to the racket and habitually surrender to it. Law surely is not the gunman situation writ large, and legal order is surely not to be thus simply identified with compulsion. . . .

Rules that confer rights, though distinct from commands, need not be moral rules or coincide with them. Rights, after all, exist under the rules of ceremonies, games, and in many other spheres regulated by rules which are irrelevant to the question of justice or what the law ought to be. Nor need rules which confer rights be just or morally good rules. The rights of a master over his slaves show us that. "Their merit or demerit," as Austin termed it, depends on how rights are distributed in society and over whom or what they are exercised. These critics indeed revealed the inadequacy of the simple notions of command and habit for the analysis of law; at many points it is apparent that the social acceptance of a rule or standard of authority (even if it is motivated only by fear or superstition or rests on inertia) must be brought into the analysis and cannot itself be reduced to the two simple terms. Yet nothing in this showed the utilitarian insistence on the distinction between the existence of law and its "merits" to be wrong.

I now turn to a distinctively American criticism of the separation of the law that is from the law that ought to be. It emerged from the critical study of the judicial process with which American jurisprudence has been on the whole so beneficially occupied. The most skeptical of these critics—the loosely named "Realists" of the 1930s —perhaps too naively accepted the conceptual framework of the natural sciences as adequate for the characterization of law and for the analysis of rule-guided action of which a living system of law at least partly consists. But they opened men's eyes to what actually goes on when courts decide cases, and the contrast they drew between the actual facts of judicial decision and the traditional terminology for describing it as if it were a wholly logical operation was usually illuminating; for in spite of some exaggeration the "Realists" made us acutely conscious of one cardinal feature of human language and human thought, emphasis on which is vital not only for the understanding of law but in areas of philosophy far beyond the confines of jurisprudence. The insight of this school may be presented in the following example. A legal rule forbids you to take a vehicle into the public park. Plainly this forbids an automobile, but what about bicycles, roller skates, toy automobiles? What about airplanes? Are these, as we say, to be called "vehicles" for the purpose of the rule or not? If we are to communicate with each other at all, and if, as in the most elementary form of law, we are to express our intentions that a certain type of behavior be regulated by rules, then the general words we use—like "vehicle" in the case I consider—must have some standard instance in which no doubts are felt about its application. There must be a core of settled meaning, but there will be, as well, a penumbra of debatable cases in which words are neither obviously applicable nor obviously ruled out. These cases will each have some features in common with the standard case; they will lack others or be accompanied by features not present in the standard case. Human invention and natural processes continually throw up such variants on the familiar, and if we are to say that these ranges of facts do or do not fall under existing rules, then the classifier must make a decision which is not dictated to him, for the facts and phenomena to which we fit our words and apply our rules are as it were *dumb*. The toy automobile cannot speak up and say, "I am a vehicle for the purpose of this legal rule," nor can the roller skates chorus, "We are not a vehicle." Fact situations do not await us neatly labeled, creased, and folded, nor is their legal classification written on them to be simply read off by the judge. Instead, in applying legal rules, someone must take the responsibility of deciding that words do or do not cover some case in hand with all the practical consequences involved in this decision.

We may call the problems which arise outside the hard core of standard instances or settled meaning "problems of the penumbra"; they are always with us whether in relation to such trivial things as the regulation of the use of the public park or in relation to the multi-dimensional generalities of a constitution. If a penumbra of uncertainty must surround all legal rules, then their application to specific cases in the penumbral area cannot be a matter of logical deduction, and so deductive reasoning, which for generations has been cherished as the very perfection of human reasoning, cannot serve as a model for what judges, or indeed anyone, should do in bringing particular cases under general rules. In this area men cannot live by deduction alone. And it follows that if legal arguments and legal decisions of penumbral questions are to be rational, their rationality must lie in something other than a logical relation to premises. So if it is rational or "sound" to argue and to decide that for the purposes of this rule an airplane is not a vehicle, this argument must be sound or rational without being logically conclusive. What is it then that makes such decisions correct or at least better than alternative decisions? Again, it seems true to say that the criterion which makes a decision sound in such cases is some concept of what the law ought to be; it is easy to slide from that into saying that it must be a moral judgment about what law ought to be. . . .

But how does the wrongness of deciding cases in an automatic and mechanical way and the rightness of deciding cases by reference to social purposes show that the utilitarian insistence on the distinction between what the law is and what it ought to be is wrong? I take it that no one who wished to use these vices of formalism as proof that the distinction between what is and what ought to be is mistaken would deny that the decisions stigmatized as automatic are law; nor would he deny that the system in which such automatic decisions are made is a legal system. Surely he would say that they are law, but they are bad law, they ought not to be law. But this would be to use the distinction, not to refute it; and of course both Bentham and Austin used it to attack judges for failing to decide penumbral cases in accordance with the growing needs of society. . . .

It does not follow that, because the opposite of a decision reached blindly in the formalist or literalist manner is a decision intelligently reached by reference to some conception of what ought to be, we have a junction of law and morals. We must, I think, beware of thinking in a too simple-minded fashion about the word "ought." This is not because there is no distinction to be made between law as it is and ought to be. Far from it. It is because the distinction should be between what is and what from many different points of view ought to be. The word "ought" merely reflects the presence of some standard of criticism; one of these standards is a moral standard but not all standards are moral. We say to our neighbor, "You ought not to lie," and that may certainly be a moral judgment, but we should remember that the baffled poisoner may say, "I ought to have given her a second dose." The point here is that intelligent decisions which we oppose to mechanical or formal decisions are not necessarily identical with decisions defensible on moral grounds. We may say of many a decision: "Yes, that is right; that is as it ought to be," and we may mean only that some accepted purpose or policy has been thereby advanced; we may not mean to endorse the moral propriety of the policy or the decision. So the contrast between the mechanical decision and the intelligent one can be reproduced inside a system dedicated to the pursuit of the most evil aims. It does not exist as a contrast to be found only in legal systems which, like our own, widely recognize principles of justice and moral claims of individuals.

An example may make this point plainer. With us the task of sentencing in criminal cases is the one that seems most obviously to demand from the judge the exercise of moral judgment. Here the factors to be weighed seem clearly to be moral factors: society must not be exposed to wanton attack; too much misery must not be inflicted on either the victim or his dependents; efforts must be made to enable him to lead a better life and regain a position in the society whose laws he has violated. To a judge striking the balance among these claims, with all the discretion and perplexities involved, his task seems as plain an example of the exercise of moral judgment as could be; and it seems to be the polar opposite of some mechanical application of a tariff of penalties fixing a sentence careless of the moral claims which in our system have to be weighed. So here intelligent and rational decision is guided however uncertainly by moral aims. But we have only to vary the example to see that this need not necessarily be so and surely, if it need not necessarily be so, the utilitarian point remains unshaken. Under the Nazi regime men were sentenced by courts for criticism of the regime. Here the choice of sentence might be guided exclusively by consideration of what was needed to maintain the state's tyranny effectively. What sentence would both terrorize the public at large and keep the friends and family of the prisoner in suspense so that both hope and fear would cooperate as factors making for subservience? The prisoner of such a system would be regarded simply as an object to be used in pursuit of these aims. Yet, in contrast with a mechanical decision, decision on these grounds would be intelligent and purposive, and from one point of view the decision would be as it ought to be. Of course, I am not unaware that a whole philosophical tradition has sought to demonstrate the fact that we cannot correctly call decisions or behavior truly rational unless they are in conformity with moral aims and principles. But the example I have used seems to me to serve at least as a warning that we cannot use the errors of formalism as something which per se demonstrates the falsity of the utilitarian insistence on the distinction between law as it is and law as *morally* it ought to be.

We can now return to the main point. If it is true that the intelligent decision of penumbral questions is one made not mechanically but in the light of aims, purposes, and policies, though not necessarily in the light of anything we would call moral principles, is it wise to express this important fact by saying that the firm utilitarian distinction be-tween what the law is and what it ought to be should be dropped? Perhaps the claim that it is wise cannot be theoretically refuted for it is, in effect, an *invitation* to revise our conception of what a legal rule is. We are invited to include in the "rule" the various aims and policies in the light of which its penumbral cases are decided on the ground that these aims have, because of their importance, as much right to be called law as the core of legal rules whose meaning is settled. But though an invitation cannot be refuted, it may be refused and I would proffer two reasons for refusing this invitation. First, everything we have learned about the judicial process can be ex-pressed in other less mysterious ways. We can say laws are incurably incomplete and we must decide the penumbral cases rationally by reference to social aims. I think Holmes, who had such a vivid appre-ciation of the fact that "general propositions do not decide concrete cases," would have put it that way. Second, to insist on the utilitarian distinction is to emphasize that the hard core of settled meaning is law in some centrally important sense and that even if there are borderlines, there must first be lines. If this were not so the notion of rules controlling courts' decisions would be senseless as some of the "Realists"—in their most extreme moods, and, I think, on bad grounds—claimed.[4]

By contrast, to soften the distinction, to assert mysteriously that there is some fused identity between law as it is and as it ought to be, is to suggest that all legal questions are fundamentally like those of the penumbra. It is to assert that there is no central element of actual law to be seen in the core of central meaning which rules have, that there is nothing in the nature of a legal rule inconsistent with *all* questions being open to reconsideration in the light of social policy. Of course, it is good to be occupied with the penumbra. Its problems are rightly the daily diet of the law schools. But to be occupied with the penumbra is one thing, to be preoccupied with it another. And preoccupation with the penumbra is, if I may say so, as rich a source of confusion in the American legal tradition as formalism in the Eng-lish. Of course we might abandon the notion that rules have author-ity; we might cease to attach force or even meaning to an argument that a case falls clearly within a rule and the scope of a precedent. We might call all such reasoning "automatic" or "mechanical," which is already the routine invective of the courts. But until we decide that this *is* what we want, we should not encourage it by obliterating the utilitarian distinction.

The third criticism of the separation of law and morals is of a very different character; it certainly is less an intellectual argument against the utilitarian distinction than a passionate appeal supported not by detailed reasoning but by reminders of a terrible experience. For it consists of the testimony of those who have descended into Hell, and, like Ulysses or Dante, brought back a message for human beings. Only in this case the Hell was not beneath or beyond earth, but on it; it was a Hell created on earth by men for other men.

This appeal comes from those German thinkers who lived through the Nazi regime and reflected upon its evil manifestations in the legal system. One of these thinkers, Gustav Radbruch, had himself shared the "positivist" doctrine until the Nazi tyranny, but he was converted by this experience and so his appeal to other men to discard the doctrine of the separation of law and morals has the special poignancy of a recantation. What is important about this criticism is that it really does confront the particular point which Bentham and Austin had in mind in urging the separation of law as it is and as it ought to be. These German thinkers put their insistence on the need to join together what the Utilitarians separated just where this separation was of most importance in the eyes of the Utilitarians; for they were concerned with the problem posed by the existence of morally evil laws. . . .

After the war Radbruch's conception of law as containing in itself the essential moral principle of humanitarianism was applied in practice by German courts in certain cases in which local war criminals, spies, and informers under the Nazi regime were punished. The special importance of these cases is that the persons accused of these crimes claimed that what they had done was not illegal under the laws of the regime in force at the time these actions were performed. This plea was met with the reply that the laws upon which they relied were invalid as contravening the fundamental principles of morality. Let me cite briefly one of these cases.[5]

In 1944 a woman, wishing to be rid of her husband, denounced him to the authorities for insulting remarks he had made about Hitler while home on leave from the German army. The wife was under no legal duty to report his acts, though what he had said was apparently in violation of statutes making it illegal to make statements detrimental to the government of the Third Reich or to impair by any means the military defense of the German people. The husband was arrested and sentenced to death, apparently pursuant to these statutes, though he was not executed but was sent to the front. In 1949 the wife was prosecuted in a West German court for an offense which we would describe as illegally depriving a person of his freedom (*rechtswidrige Freiheitsberaubung*). This was punishable as a crime under the German Criminal Code of 1871 which had remained in force continuously since its enactment. The wife pleaded that her husband's imprisonment was pursuant to the Nazi statutes and hence that she had committed no crime. The court of appeal to which the case ultimately came held that the wife was guilty of procuring the deprivation of her husband's liberty by denouncing him to the German courts, even though he had been sentenced by a court for having violated a statute, since, to quote the words of the court, the statute "was contrary to the sound conscience and sense of justice of all decent human beings." This reasoning was followed in many cases which have been hailed as a triumph of the doctrines of natural law and as signaling the overthrow of positivism. The unqualified satisfaction with this result seems to me to be hysteria. Many of us might applaud the objective—that of punishing a woman for an outrageously immoral act—but this was secured only by declaring a statute established since 1934 not to have the force of law, and at least the wisdom of this course must be doubted. There were, of course, two other choices. One was to let the woman go unpunished; one can sympathize with and endorse the view that this might have been a bad thing to do. The other was to face the fact that if the woman were to be punished it must be pursuant to the introduction of a frankly retrospective law and with a full consciousness of what was sacrificed in securing her punishment in this way. Odious as retrospective criminal legislation and punishment may be, to have pursued it openly in this case would at least have had the merits of candor. It would have made plain that in punishing the woman a choice had to be made between two evils, that of leaving her unpunished and that of sacrificing a very precious principle of morality endorsed by most legal systems. Surely if we have learned anything from the history of morals it is that the thing to do with a moral quandary is not to hide it. Like nettles, the occasions when life forces us to choose between the lesser of two evils must be grasped with the consciousness that they are what they are. . . .

It may seem perhaps to make too much of forms, even perhaps of words, to emphasize one way of disposing of this difficult case as compared with another which might have led, so far as the woman was concerned, to exactly the same result. Why should we dramatize the difference between them? We might punish the woman under a new retrospective law and declare overtly that we were doing something inconsistent with our principles as the lesser of two evils; or we might allow the case to pass as one in which we do not point out precisely where we sacrifice such a principle. But candor is not just one among many minor virtues of the administration of law, just as it is not merely a minor virtue of morality. For if we adopt Radbruch's view, and with him and the German courts make our protest against evil law in the form of an assertion that certain rules cannot be law because of their moral iniquity, we confuse one of the most powerful, because it is the simplest, forms of moral criticism. If with the Utilitarians we speak plainly, we say that laws may be law but too evil to be obeyed. This is a moral condemnation which everyone can understand and it makes an immediate and obvious claim to moral attention. If, on the other hand, we formulate our objection as an assertion that these evil things are not law, here is an assertion which many people do not believe, and if they are disposed to consider it at all, it would seem to raise a whole host of philosophical issues before it can be accepted. So perhaps the most important single lesson to be learned from this form of the denial of the utilitarian distinction is the one that the Utilitarians were most concerned to teach: when we have the ample resources of plain speech we must not present the moral criticism of institutions as propositions of a disputable philosophy. . . .

Another aspect of the matter deserves attention. If we attach to a legal system the minimum meaning that it must consist of general rules—general both in the sense that they refer to courses of action, not single actions, and to multiplicities of men, not single individuals—this meaning connotes the principle of treating like cases alike, though the criteria of when cases are alike will be, so far, only the general elements specified in the rules. It is, however, true that *one* essential element of the concept of justice is the principle of treating like cases alike. This is justice in the administration of the law, not justice of the law. So there is, in the very notion of law consisting of general rules, something which prevents us from treating it as if morally it is utterly neutral, without any necessary contact with moral principles. Natural procedural justice consists therefore of those principles of objectivity and impartiality in the administration of the law which implement just this aspect of law and which are designed to ensure that rules are applied only to what are genuinely cases of the rule or at least to minimize the risks of inequalities in this sense.

[This reason] for talking of a certain overlap between legal and moral standards as necessary and natural, of course, should not satisfy anyone who is really disturbed by the utilitarian or "positivist" insistence that law and morality are distinct. This is so because a legal system that satisfied these minimum requirements might apply, with the most pedantic impartiality as between the persons affected, laws which were hideously oppressive, and might deny to a vast rightless slave population the minimum benefits of protection from violence and theft. The stink of such societies is, after all, still in our nostrils and to argue that they have (or had) no legal system would only involve the repetition of the argument. Only if the rules failed to provide these essential benefits and protection for anyone—even for a slave-owning group—would the minimum be unsatisfied and the system sink to the status of a set of meaningless taboos. Of course no one denied those benefits would have any reason to obey except fear and would have every moral reason to revolt. . . .

NOTES

1. John Austin, *The Province of Jurisprudence Determined* (Library of Ideas ed., 1954) 102 n. 12.

2. Jeremy Bentham, *A Fragment on Government,* in *The Works of Jeremy Bentham,* ed. John Bowring (Edinburgh: W. Tait, 1859) 1:221, 289–90 (c. IV, paragraphs 33–34).

3. See Austin, 231 n. 1.

4. One recantation of this extreme position is worth mention in the present context. In the first edition of *The Bramble Bush,* Karl N. Llewellyn committed himself wholeheartedly to the view that "what these officials do about disputes is, to my mind, the law itself" and that "*rules* . . . are important so far as they help you . . . predict what judges will do. . . . That is all their importance, except as pretty playthings" (*The Bramble Bush* [1st ed.; 1930] 3, 5). In the second edition he said that these were "unhappy words when not more fully developed, and they are plainly at best a very partial statement of the whole truth. . . . [O]ne office of law is to control officials in some part, and to guide them even . . . where no thoroughgoing control is possible, or is desired. . . . [T]he words fail to take proper account . . . of the office of the institution of law as an instrument of conscious shaping . . ." (*The Bramble Bush* [2d ed.; 1951] 9).

5. Judgment of 27 July 1949, Oberlandesgericht, Bamberg, 5 *Süddeutsche Juristen-Zeitung* (Germany, 1950) 207; *Harvard Law Review* 64 (1951) 1005. See Wolfgang Gaston Friedman, *Legal Theory* (3d ed., London: Stevens & Sons, 1953) 457.

5

Positivism and Fidelity to Law—A Reply to Professor Hart*

Lon L. Fuller

The Moral Foundations of a Legal Order

Professor Hart emphatically rejects "the command theory of law," according to which law is simply a command backed by a force sufficient to make it effective. He observes that such a command can be given by a man with a loaded gun, and "law surely is not the gunman situation writ large." There is no need to dwell here on the inadequacies of the command theory, since Professor Hart has already revealed its defects more clearly and succinctly than I could. His conclusion is that the foundation of a legal system is not coercive power, but certain "fundamental accepted rules specifying the essential lawmaking procedures."

When I reached this point in his essay, I felt certain that Professor Hart was about to acknowledge an important qualification on his thesis. I confidently expected that he would go on to say something like this: I have insisted throughout on the importance of keeping sharp the distinction between law and morality. The question may now be raised, therefore, as to the nature of these fundamental rules that furnish the framework within which the making of law takes place. On the one hand, they seem to be rules, not of law, but of morality. They derive their efficacy from a general acceptance, which

*First published in *Harvard Law Review* 71 (1958) 630–72.

in turn rests ultimately on a perception that they are right and necessary. They can hardly be said to be law in the sense of an authoritative pronouncement, since their function is to state when a pronouncement is authoritative. On the other hand, in the daily functioning of the legal system they are often treated and applied much as ordinary rules of law are. Here, then, we must confess there is something that can be called a "merger" of law and morality, and to which the term "intersection" is scarcely appropriate.

Instead of pursuing some such course of thought, to my surprise I found Professor Hart leaving completely untouched the nature of the fundamental rules that make law itself possible, and turning his attention instead to what he considers a confusion of thought on the part of the critics of positivism. . . .

The Morality of Law Itself

Most of the issues raised by Professor Hart's essay can be restated in terms of the distinction between order and good order. Law may be said to represent order *simpliciter*. Good order is law that corresponds to the demands of justice, or morality, or men's notions of what ought to be. This rephrasing of the issue is useful in bringing to light the ambitious nature of Professor Hart's undertaking, for surely we would all agree that it is no easy thing to distinguish order from good order. When it is said, for example, that law simply represents that public order which obtains under all governments—democratic, Fascist, or Communist[1]—the order intended is certainly not that of a morgue or cemetery. We must mean a functioning order, and such an order has to be at least good enough to be considered as functioning by some standard or other. A reminder that workable order usually requires some play in the joints, and therefore cannot be too orderly, is enough to suggest some of the complexities that would be involved in any attempt to draw a sharp distinction between order and good order.

For the time being, however, let us suppose we can in fact clearly separate the concept of order from that of good order. Even in this unreal and abstract form the notion of order itself contains what may be called a moral element. Let me illustrate this "morality of order" in its crudest and most elementary form. Let us suppose an absolute monarch, whose word is the only law known to his subjects. We may further suppose him to be utterly selfish and to seek in his relations with his subjects solely his own advantage. This monarch from time to time issues commands, promising rewards for compliance and threatening punishment for disobedience. He is, however, a dissolute and forgetful fellow, who never makes the slightest attempt to ascertain who have in fact followed his directions and who have not. As a result he habitually punishes loyalty and rewards disobedience. It is apparent that this monarch will never achieve even his own selfish aims until he is ready to accept that minimum self-restraint that will create a meaningful connection between his words and his actions.

Let us now suppose that our monarch undergoes a change of heart and begins to pay some attention to what he said yesterday when, today, he has occasion to distribute bounty or to order the chopping off of heads. Under the strain of this new responsibility, however, our monarch relaxes his attention in other directions and becomes hopelessly slothful in the phrasing of his commands. His orders become so ambiguous and are uttered in so inaudible a tone that his subjects never have any clear idea what he wants them to do. Here, again, it is apparent that if our monarch for his own selfish advantage wants to create in his realm anything like a system of law he will have to pull himself together and assume still another responsibility.

Law, considered merely as order, contains, then, its own implicit morality. This morality of order must be respected if we are to create anything that can be called law, even bad law. Law by itself is powerless to bring this morality into existence. Until our monarch is really ready to face the responsibilities of his position, it will do no good for him to issue still another futile command, this time self-addressed and threatening himself with punishment if he does not mend his ways.

There is a twofold sense in which it is true that law cannot be built on law. First of all, the authority to make law must be supported by moral attitudes that accord to it the competency it claims. Here we are dealing with a morality external to law, which makes law possible. But this alone is not enough. We may stipulate that in our monarchy the accepted "basic norm" designates the monarch himself as the only possible source of law. We still cannot have law until our monarch is ready to accept the internal morality of law itself.

In the life of a nation these external and internal moralities of law reciprocally influence one another; a deterioration of the one will almost inevitably produce a deterioration in the other. So closely related are they that when the anthropologist Lowie speaks of "the generally accepted ethical postulates underlying our . . . legal institutions as their ultimate sanction and guaranteeing their smooth functioning,"[2] he may be presumed to have both of them in mind.

What I have called "the internal morality of law" seems to be almost completely neglected by Professor Hart. He does make brief mention of "justice in the administration of the law," which consists in the like treatment of like cases, by whatever elevated or perverted standards the word "like" may be defined. But he quickly dismisses this aspect of law as having no special relevance to his main enterprise.

In this I believe he is profoundly mistaken. It is his neglect to analyze the demands of a morality of order that leads him throughout his essay to treat law as a datum projecting itself into human experience and not as an object of human striving. When we realize that order itself is something that must be worked for, it becomes apparent that the existence of a legal system, even a bad or evil legal system, is always a matter of degree. When we recognize this simple fact of everyday legal experience, it becomes impossible to dismiss the problems presented by the Nazi regime with a simple assertion: "Under the Nazis there was law, even if it was bad law." We have instead to inquire how much of a legal system survived the general debasement and perversion of all forms of social order that occurred under the Nazi rule, and what moral implications this mutilated system had for the conscientious citizen forced to live under it. . . .

The Problem of Restoring Respect for Law and Justice After the Collapse of a Regime That Respected Neither

After the collapse of the Nazi regime the German courts were faced with a truly frightful predicament. It was impossible for them to declare the whole dictatorship illegal or to treat as void every decision and legal enactment that had emanated from Hitler's government. Intolerable dislocations would have resulted from any such wholesale outlawing of all that occurred over a span of twelve years. On the other hand, it was equally impossible to carry forward into the new government the effects of every Nazi perversity that had been committed in the name of law; any such course would have tainted an indefinite future with the poisons of Nazism.

This predicament—which was, indeed, a pervasive one, affecting all branches of law—came to a dramatic head in a series of cases involving informers who had taken advantage of the Nazi terror to get rid of personal enemies or unwanted spouses. If all Nazi statutes and judicial decisions were indiscriminately "law," then these despicable creatures were guiltless, since they had turned their victims over to processes which the Nazis themselves knew by the name of law. Yet it was intolerable, especially for the surviving relatives and friends of the victims, that these people should go about unpunished, while the objects of their spite were dead, or were just being released after years of imprisonment, or, more painful still, simply remained unaccounted for.

The urgency of this situation does not by any means escape Professor Hart. Indeed, he is moved to recommend an expedient that is surely not lacking itself in a certain air of desperation. He suggests that a retroactive criminal statute would have been the least objectionable solution to the problem. This statute would have punished the informer, and branded him as a criminal, for an act which Professor Hart regards as having been perfectly legal when he committed it.

On the other hand, Professor Hart condemns without qualification those judicial decisions in which the courts themselves undertook to declare void certain of the Nazi statutes under which the informer's victims had been convicted. One cannot help raising at this point the question whether the issue as presented by Professor Hart himself is truly that of fidelity to law. Surely it would be a necessary implication of a retroactive criminal statute against informers that, for purposes of that statute at least, the Nazi laws as applied to the informers or their victims were to be regarded as void. With this turn the question seems no longer to be whether what was once law can now be declared not to have been law, but rather who should do the dirty work, the courts or the legislature.

But, as Professor Hart himself suggests, the issues at stake are much too serious to risk losing them in a semantic tangle. Even if the whole question were one of words, we should remind ourselves that we are in an area where words have a powerful effect on human attitudes. I should like, therefore, to undertake a defense of the German courts, and to advance reasons why, in my opinion, their decisions do not represent the abandonment of legal principle that Professor Hart sees in them. In order to understand the background of those decisions we shall have to move a little closer within smelling distance of the witches' caldron than we have been brought so far by Professor Hart. We shall have also to consider an aspect of the problem ignored in his essay, namely, the degree to which the Nazis observed what I have called the inner morality of law itself.

Throughout his discussion Professor Hart seems to assume that the only difference between Nazi law and, say, English law is that the

Nazis used their laws to achieve ends that are odious to an Englishman. This assumption is, I think, seriously mistaken, and Professor Hart's acceptance of it seems to me to render his discussion unresponsive to the problem it purports to address.

Throughout their period of control the Nazis took generous advantage of a device not wholly unknown to American legislatures, the retroactive statute curing past legal irregularities. The most dramatic use of the curative powers of such a statute occurred on July 3, 1934, after the "Roehm purge." When this intraparty shooting affair was over and more than seventy Nazis had been—one can hardly avoid saying—"rubbed out," Hitler returned to Berlin and procured from his cabinet a law ratifying and confirming the measures taken between June 30 and July 1, 1934, without mentioning the names of those who were now considered to have been lawfully executed.[3] Some time later Hitler declared that during the Roehm purge "the supreme court of the German people . . . consisted of myself,"[4] surely not an overstatement of the capacity in which he acted if one takes seriously the enactment conferring retroactive legality on "the measures taken."

Now in England and America it would never occur to anyone to say that "it is in the nature of law that it cannot be retroactive," although, of course, constitutional inhibitions may prohibit certain kinds of retroactivity. We would say it is normal for a law to operate prospectively, and that it may be arguable that it ought never operate otherwise, but there would be a certain occult unpersuasiveness in any assertion that retroactivity violates the very nature of law itself. Yet we have only to imagine a country in which *all* laws are retroactive in order to see that retroactivity presents a real problem for the internal morality of law. If we suppose an absolute monarch who allows his realm to exist in a constant state of anarchy, we would hardly say that he could create a regime of law simply by enacting a curative statute conferring legality on everything that had happened up to its date and by announcing an intention to enact similar statutes every six months in the future.

A general increase in the resort to statutes curative of past legal irregularities represents a deterioration in that form of legal morality without which law itself cannot exist. The threat of such statutes hangs over the whole legal system, and robs every law on the books of some of its significance. And surely a general threat of this sort is implied when a government is willing to use such a statute to transform into lawful execution what was simple murder when it happened.

During the Nazi regime there were repeated rumors of "secret laws." In the article criticized by Professor Hart, Radbruch mentions a report that the wholesale killings in concentration camps were made "lawful" by a secret enactment.[5] Now surely there can be no greater legal monstrosity than a secret statute. Would anyone seriously recommend that following the war the German courts should have searched for unpublished laws among the files left by Hitler's government so that citizens' rights could be determined by a reference to these laws?

The extent of the legislator's obligation to make his laws known to his subjects is, of course, a problem of legal morality that has been under active discussion at least since the Secession of the Plebs. There is probably no modern state that has not been plagued by this problem in one form or another. It is most likely to arise in modern societies with respect to unpublished administrative directions. Often these are regarded in quite good faith by those who issue them as affecting only matters of internal organization. But since the procedures followed by an administrative agency, even in its "internal" actions, may seriously affect the rights and interests of the citizen, these unpublished, or "secret," regulations are often a subject for complaint.

But as with retroactivity, what in most societies is kept under control by the tacit restraints of legal decency broke out in monstrous form under Hitler. Indeed, so loose was the whole Nazi morality of law that it is not easy to know just what should be regarded as an unpublished or secret law. Since unpublished instructions to those administering the law could destroy the letter of any published law by imposing on it an outrageous interpretation, there was a sense in which the meaning of every law was "secret." Even a verbal order from Hitler that a thousand prisoners in concentration camps be put to death was at once an administrative direction and a validation of everything done under it as being "lawful."

But the most important affronts to the morality of law by Hitler's government took no such subtle forms as those exemplified in the bizarre outcroppings I have just discussed. In the first place, when legal forms became inconvenient, it was always possible for the Nazis to bypass them entirely and "to act through the party in the streets." There was no one who dared bring them to account for whatever outrages might thus be committed. In the second place, the Nazi-dominated courts were always ready to disregard any statute, even those enacted by the Nazis themselves, if this suited their convenience or if they feared that a lawyer-like interpretation might incur displeasure "above."

This complete willingness of the Nazis to disregard even their own enactments was an important factor leading Radbruch to take the position he did in the articles so severely criticized by Professor Hart. I do not believe that any fair appraisal of the action of the postwar German courts is possible unless we take this factor into account, as Professor Hart fails completely to do.

These remarks may seem inconclusive in their generality and to rest more on assertion than evidentiary fact. Let us turn at once, then, to the actual case discussed by Professor Hart.[6]

In 1944 a German soldier paid a short visit to his wife while under travel orders on a reassignment. During the single day he was home, he conveyed privately to his wife something of his opinion of the Hitler government. He expressed disapproval of (*sich abfällig geäussert über*) Hitler and other leading personalities of the Nazi party. He also said it was too bad Hitler had not met his end in the assassination attempt that had occurred on July 20th of that year. Shortly after his departure, his wife, who during his long absence on military duty "had turned to other men" and who wished to get rid of him, reported his remarks to the local leader of the Nazi party, observing that "a man who would say a thing like that does not deserve to live." The result was a trial of the husband by a military tribunal and a sentence of death. After a short period of imprisonment, instead of being executed, he was sent to the front again. After the collapse of the Nazi regime, the wife was brought to trial for having procured the imprisonment of her husband. Her defense rested on the ground that her husband's statements to her about Hitler and the Nazis constituted a crime under the laws then in force. Accordingly, when she informed on her husband she was simply bringing a criminal to justice.

This defense rested on two statutes, one passed in 1934, the other in 1938. Let us first consider the second of these enactments, which was part of a more comprehensive legislation creating a whole series of special wartime criminal offenses. I reproduce below a translation of the only pertinent section:

> The following persons are guilty of destroying the national power of resistance and shall be punished by death: Whoever publicly solicits or incites a refusal to fulfill the obligations of service in the armed forces of Germany, or in armed forces allied with Germany, or who otherwise publicly seeks to injure or destroy the will of the German people or an allied people to assert themselves stalwartly against their enemies.[7]

It is almost inconceivable that a court of present-day Germany would hold the husband's remarks to his wife, who was barred from military duty by her sex, to be a violation of the final catchall provision of this statute, particularly when it is recalled that the text reproduced above was part of a more comprehensive enactment dealing with such things as harboring deserters, escaping military duty by self-inflicted injuries, and the like. The question arises, then, as to the extent to which the interpretive principles applied by the courts of Hitler's government should be accepted in determining whether the husband's remarks were indeed unlawful.

This question becomes acute when we note that the act applies only to *public* acts or utterances, whereas the husband's remarks were in the privacy of his own home. Now it appears that the Nazi courts (and it should be noted we are dealing with a special military court) quite generally disregarded this limitation and extended the act to all utterances, private or public.[8] Is Professor Hart prepared to say that the legal meaning of this statute is to be determined in the light of this apparently uniform principle of judicial interpretation?

Let us turn now to the other statute upon which Professor Hart relies in assuming that the husband's utterance was unlawful. This is the act of 1934, the relevant portions of which are translated below:

(1) Whoever publicly makes spiteful or provocative statements directed against, or statements which disclose a base disposition toward, the leading personalities of the nation or of the National Socialist German Workers' Party, or toward measures taken or institutions established by them, and of such a nature as to undermine the people's confidence in their political leadership, shall be punished by imprisonment.

(2) Malicious utterances not made in public shall be treated in the same manner as public utterances when the person making them realized or should have realized they would reach the public.

(3) Prosecution for such utterances shall be only on the order of the National Minister of Justice; in case the utterance was directed against a leading personality of the National Socialist German Workers' Party, the Minister of Justice shall order prosecution only with the advice and consent of the Representative of the Leader.

(4) The National Minister of Justice shall, with the advice and consent of the Representative of the Leader, determine who shall belong to the class of leading personalities for purposes of Section 1 above.[9]

Extended comment on this legislative monstrosity is scarcely called for, overlarded and undermined as it is by uncontrolled administrative discretion. We may note only: first, that it offers no justification whatever for the death penalty actually imposed on the husband, though never carried out; second, that if the wife's act in informing on her husband made his remarks "public," there is no such thing as a private utterance under this statute. I should like to ask the reader whether he can actually share Professor Hart's indignation that, in the perplexities of the postwar reconstruction, the German courts saw fit to declare this thing not a law. Can it be argued seriously that it would have been more beseeming to the judicial process if the postwar courts had undertaken a study of "the interpretative principles" in force during Hitler's rule and had then solemnly applied those "principles" to ascertain the meaning of this statute? On the other hand, would the courts really have been showing respect for Nazi law if they had construed the Nazi statutes by their own, quite different, standards of interpretation?

Professor Hart castigates the German courts and Radbruch, not so much for what they believed had to be done, but because they failed to see that they were confronted by a moral dilemma of a sort that would have been immediately apparent to Bentham and Austin. By the simple dodge of saying, "When a statute is sufficiently evil it ceases to be law," they ran away from the problem they should have faced.

This criticism is, I believe, without justification. So far as the courts are concerned, matters certainly would not have been helped if, instead of saying, "This is not law," they had said, "This is law but it is so evil we will refuse to apply it." Surely moral confusion reaches its height when a court refuses to apply something it admits to be law, and Professor Hart does not recommend any such "facing of the true issue" by the courts themselves. He would have preferred a retroactive statute. Curiously, this was also the preference of Radbruch. But unlike Professor Hart, the German courts and Gustav Radbruch were living participants in a situation of drastic emergency. The informer problem was a pressing one, and if legal institutions were to be rehabilitated in Germany it would not do to allow the people to begin taking the law into their own hands, as might have occurred while the courts were waiting for a statute. . . .

I hope I am not being unjust to Professor Hart when I say that I can find no way of describing the dilemma as he sees it but to use some such words as the following: On the one hand, we have an amoral datum called law, which has the peculiar quality of creating a moral duty to obey it. On the other hand, we have a moral duty to do what we think is right and decent. When we are confronted by a statute we believe to be thoroughly evil, we have to choose between those two duties.

If this is the positivist position, then I have no hesitancy in rejecting it. The "dilemma" it states has the verbal formulation of a problem, but the problem it states makes no sense. It is like saying I have to choose between giving food to a starving man and being mimsy with the borogoves. I do not think it is unfair to the positivistic philosophy to say that it never gives any coherent meaning to the moral obligation of fidelity to law. This obligation seems to be conceived as sui generis, wholly unrelated to any of the ordinary, extralegal ends of human life. The fundamental postulate of positivism—that law must be strictly severed from morality—seems to deny the possibility of any bridge between the obligation to obey law and other moral obligations. No mediating principle can measure their respective demands on conscience, for they exist in wholly separate worlds.

While I would not subscribe to all of Radbruch's postwar views—especially those relating to "higher law"—I think he saw, much more clearly than does Professor Hart, the true nature of the dilemma confronted by Germany in seeking to rebuild her shattered legal institutions. Germany had to restore both respect for law and respect for justice. Though neither of these could be restored without the other, painful antinomies were encountered in attempting to restore both at once, as Radbruch saw all too clearly. Essentially Radbruch saw the dilemma as that of meeting the demands of order, on the one hand, and those of good order, on the other. Of course no pat formula can be derived from this phrasing of the problem. But, unlike legal positivism, it does not present us with opposing demands that have no living contact with one another, that simply shout their contradictions across a vacuum. As we seek order, we can meaningfully remind ourselves that order itself will do us no good unless it is good for something. As we seek to make our order good, we can remind ourselves that justice itself is impossible without order, and that we must not lose order itself in the attempt to make it good. . . .

To me there is nothing shocking in saying that a dictatorship which clothes itself with a tinsel of legal form can so far depart from the morality of order, from the inner morality of law itself, that it ceases to be a legal system. When a system calling itself law is predicated upon a general disregard by judges of the terms of the laws they purport to enforce, when this system habitually cures its legal irregularities, even the grossest, by retroactive statutes, when it has only to resort to forays of terror in the streets, which no one dares challenge, in order to escape even those scant restraints imposed by the pretense of legality—when all these things have become true of a dictatorship, it is not hard for me, at least, to deny to it the name of law. . . .

NOTES

1. For example, Wolfgang Gaston Friedmann, "The Planned State and the Rule of Law," *Australian Law Journal* 22 (1948) 162, 207.

2. Robert Harry Lowie, *The Origin of the State* (New York: Harcourt, Brace & Co., 1927) 113.

3. *New York Times,* 4 July 1934 (late city edition) p. 3.

4. See *New York Times,* 14 July 1934 (late city edition) p. 5.

5. Gustav Radbruch, "Die Erneuerung des Rechts," *Die Wandlung* 2 (1947) 8, 9. A useful discussion of the Nazi practice with reference to the publicity given laws will be found in Friedrich Giese, "Verkündung und Gesetzeskraft," *Archiv des Öffentlichen Rechts* 76 (1951) 464, 471–72. I rely on this article for the remarks that follow in the text.

6. Judgment of 27 July 1949, Oberlandesgericht, Bamberg, 5 *Süddeutsche Juristen-Zeitung* (1950) 207; *Harvard Law Review* 64 (1951) 1005.

7. The passage translated is section 5 of a statute creating a Kriegssonder-strafrecht. Law of 17 August 1938, (1939) 2 *Reichsgesetzblatt* pt. I, at 1456. The translation is mine.

8. See 5 *Süddeutsche Juristen-Zeitung* (1950) 207, 210.

9. The translated passage is article 2 of A Law Against Malicious Attacks on the State and the Party and for the Protection of the Party Uniform. Law of 20 December 1934, (1934) 1 *Reichsgesetzblatt* 1269. The translation is mine.

6

Three Contexts of Law *

Douglas Sturm

It has been observed by Alan Gewirth that "jurisprudence, the science of law, has always been beset by . . . categorial problems."[1] This is another way of saying that men who talk about law are never quite sure what it is they are talking about. Of course, the central categorial problem of jurisprudence is encapsulated in the question, What is law? The vast literature that is devoted to this question is, as might be expected, highly abstract, so much so that ofttimes legal practitioners pass it off with a flick of the wrist as completely irrelevant to the practical tasks of law. One reason that the question is so doggedly persistent, however, is the suspicion that legal practice cannot completely escape legal theory. What the jurist does expresses how the jurist understands. Even if the legal practitioner does not concern himself explicitly with the categorial question of jurisprudence, the style of his practice will bear witness more or less clearly to his actual, albeit implicit, comprehension of legal realities.

The manner in which one comprehends law depends in large part upon perspective, and perspective depends in large part upon the context of one's observations. There are perhaps an untold number of perspectives and an untold number of contexts. I shall confine this discussion to three contexts, all of which supply fruitful and interesting modes of understanding, interpreting, and even evaluating law. No one of these contexts is sufficient; each tends to shade off into the

---

*First published in *Journal of Religion* 47 (1964) 127–45.

others; all accentuate what in the others is subdued. The three contexts are the strictly legal, the social, and the religious-humanistic.

Strictly Legal Context

Surely H. L. A. Hart's book *The Concept of Law* (1961)[2] is one of
the clearest and most persuasively argued attempts of recent times to
solve the central categorial problem of jurisprudence.[3] Hart's design
in this book is to exhibit clearly the distinctive structure of a legal
system. He rejects the possibility of a complete, exhaustive, absolutely adequate definition, and intends only to isolate the central
elements of the concept of law. Perhaps it would not be unfair to
ascribe to him the intention of delineating an understanding of law
within a strictly legal context. In doing so, he skillfully distinguishes
his own position from both Austinianism, which focuses on coercion
as the essential key to the understanding of law, and Thomism, which
claims to discover a necessary connection between law and morality.
Without ignoring the sundry infusions of coercion and morality into
a legal system, Hart seeks to rescue law from the reductionism of the
gunman metaphor and to set forth law in its essentially non-moral—
and a fortiori non-religious—meaning.

Contrary to the Austinian position, Hart finds the proper key to
the science of law in the idea of a rule. But what exactly is a rule? In
Hart's usage, a rule[4] is, most simply put, a standard of behavior or
conduct. Various classifications of rules are possible. Rules may be
distinguished, for example, as to whether they are taken to imply
obligation. Rules of grammar and etiquette are not; rules of morality
and law are. There are three qualities that distinguish rules of obligation from other rules, although these qualities are of such a character
that no exact and rigorous boundary line can be drawn.

The primary quality is a matter of the seriousness and the scope
of the demand that conduct conform to the rule. If a large number of
persons within a population is sufficiently serious about a rule that
criticism, hostility, and even physical sanction are characteristic reactions to actual or threatened deviation from it, then, in Hart's formulation, that rule is a rule of obligation. It is evident that this quality
is imprecise. How large is a large number? What amount of criticism,
etc., constitutes a characteristic reaction? As we shall see, the very
imprecision of this quality is one of the forces that underlies the
formation of a legal system.

The other two qualities of a rule of obligation are correlatives of
the first. Belief that conformity to the rule is indispensable for the

maintenance of the society or some important aspect of it and cognizance of the need often to renounce alternative private desires in order to adhere to the rule both support the seriousness that gives rise to obligation.

Thus general social pressure, social importance, and conflict with personal wishes specify a rule of obligation, and laws are among the rules of obligation. But obligatoriness so defined is not the most crucial characteristic of law.

Theoretically a society is possible in which the *sole* means of social control consists of "primary rules of obligation," or what Eugen Ehrlich designates the "living law."[5] Hart avers that such a society could exist satisfactorily only on the basis of three conditions. First, the rules must restrict behavior that is detrimental (such as violence, theft, and deception) and exact behavior that is contributory to social existence. Second, the majority of the members of the society must willingly accept the rules. And, third, the society must be homogeneous in sentiment and belief, and must exist within a stable environment.

Seldom do such conditions coexist; more likely, difficulties and conflicts will force upon the people methods of social control that supplement and reinforce the primary rules of conduct. Specifically, doubts will be expressed as to the status of a particular rule—is it or is it not a matter of obligation? Circumstances will shift in character, creating anachronisms among the rules and giving rise to a need for new rules. Disputes will occur over whether a rule has in fact been violated. Whether, in the history of a people, the methods of relieving these difficulties are always deliberately shaped specifically for that purpose is perhaps an open question, a question which Hart does not raise.

In any case, the dominant means of mitigating these social ills is the formation of secondary rules of obligation. This conception— of the secondary rules of obligation—is the crux of Hart's theory of law. There are three functions that are fulfilled by this supplemental method of controlling and organizing society. Rules of recognition specify the authoritative means by which the primary rules of the society are identifiable. Rules of change specify the authoritative means by which new primary rules can be introduced and old ones modified or eliminated. Rules of adjudication specify the authoritative means by which it can be decided whether a primary rule has been violated and under what conditions penalties may be applied.

The formation of rules of recognition, change, and adjudication within a society is of utmost significance; it constitutes, in Hart's words, "a step from the prelegal into the legal world";[6] it "converts the regime of primary rules into what is indisputably a legal system."[7] There is, of course, nothing inherently erroneous or immoral in using the term "law" with a broader signification. But given the fact that there is an appreciable difference between a society without and a society with secondary rules of obligation, it is useful and illuminating to reserve the term "law" to designate the union of primary and secondary rules of obligation.

To summarize the analysis of the strictly legal meaning of law to this point: laws are rules; more precisely, they are rules of obligation; and even more precisely, they consist in a conjunction of primary and secondary rules of obligation.

But, to pursue the analysis one more level: at the point of the emergence of a legal system, a new dimension seems to be added to obligation, a dimension which is denominated the "internal aspect" of law by Hart. As Clifford Pannam has written about Hart's construction, "without an appreciation of the internal aspect of legal rules, little progress will be made in understanding how law functions in a society."[8] Legal rules as such possess an internal aspect in the sense that they are *meant* to be matters of obligation, they are *meant* to be binding, they are *intended* to be assumed as matters of voluntary responsibility. But there are two divergent ways to view a legal rule or a system of legal rules—internally and externally. The external point of view is that of an observer, a spectator, an outsider, one who chooses not to "play the game." From this point of view the rules are not perceived as a matter of obligation. The internal point of view is that of a participant, an insider, a member, one to whom the rules are perceived as a matter of obligation. From this point of view legal rules are perceived as such, that is, according to their internal aspect. When legal rules are apprehended internally within a group of people, then they function "as guides to the conduct of social life, as the basis for claims, demands, admissions, criticism, or punishment . . . in all the familiar transactions of life."[9]

The terms "internal aspect" and "obligatoriness" are interchangeable in Hart's usage. To say that laws possess an internal aspect is to say that laws are intrinsically obligatory. But, of course, not everyone *accepts* laws as laws. Acceptance is crucial in the effectuation of a legal system. The word "acceptance" recurs again and again and again throughout Hart's text without special analysis, but its importance is clear. From the internal perspective, laws are accepted as laws; from the external perspective, they are not. And, Hart asserts, within any given society at any given time there will in all likelihood exist "a tension between those who, on the one hand, accept and voluntarily co-operate in maintaining the rules, and so see their own and other persons' behavior in terms of the rules, and those who, on the other hand, reject the rules and attend to them only from the external point of view as a sign of possible punishment."[10]

On this basis, a continuous scale might be constructed along which to plot legal systems according to their degree of actual effectiveness, strength, or perhaps even "health," a term which Hart employs at least once in this connection.[11] The scale would range between the termini of full and complete acceptance and full and complete rejection or non-acceptance. I resist any comment about the difficulties of ascertaining degrees of acceptance and rejection within a society, although clearly this is a matter of some moment when complaints are raised about dissatisfaction with the administration of justice or an increasing lack of respect for law.

But Hart's analysis of the components of a legal system's existence and health is more complex. He distinguishes between mere obedience and acceptance. While acceptance entails at least the intention to obey, obedience is possible without acceptance. One may obey a legal rule only because of threat of penalty, or out of inertia, or to put on the appearance of a law-abiding citizen. With that distinction between obedience and acceptance, he argues that there are two conditions necessary and sufficient for a legal system's existence. The primary rules of conduct identified as valid according to the rule of recognition must be generally *obeyed,* and the secondary rules— of recognition, of change, and of adjudication—must be *accepted* by the officials of the system. When citizens merely obey without acceptance and officials accept, then a legal system exists, but that is all. Beyond this, Hart suggests in passing, but without amplification, the possibility of a "healthy" existence where acceptance is characteristic generally of an entire population, citizens and officials.

Actually Hart devotes more space to pathological than to normal or healthy legal systems. There is a broad range of diseased conditions, depending on the particular degree and the precise combination of disobedience among citizens and unity or disunity in the matter of acceptance among officials.[12] Consequently it is possible, and fruitful, even within this strictly legal context, to view a legal system as an organism. So, Hart writes, "it becomes apparent that a legal system, like a human being, may at one stage be unborn, at a second not wholly independent of its mother, then enjoy a healthy independent existence, later decay and finally die."[13]

But "the stage at which it is right to say . . . that the legal system has finally ceased to exist is a thing not susceptible of any exact determination."[14] In part this is the case because the various primary and secondary rules of a legal system are not equivalent. To continue the biological metaphor, the rule of recognition is the very heart of the organism. Wherever a secondary rule of recognition is accepted and therefore used to identify primary rules of obligation, there a legal system has emerged, however weak and however short-lived it might be.

Thus according to Hart, the acceptance of a rule of recognition is the sine qua non of law. But, curiously, the rule of recognition of a system is often an elusive, even a fugitive, thing. It defies discovery and escapes clear definition. While a rule of recognition may consist of a single principle (e.g., decree by a king), it will more likely consist of multiple and not always consistent principles (e.g., location in an authoritative text, enactment by a legislature, decision by a court, a matter of customary practice), although one of the principles may be supreme. Moreover, the rule of recognition is seldom explicitly formulated. And in a complex society, most citizens will have barely the faintest notion of this rule of all rules. In addition, the rule of recognition, or some aspect of it, may be of exceedingly ambiguous and doubtful meaning. However, while the rule of recognition of a given legal system may be complex, unformulated, unknown, uncertain and open-textured, it nonetheless constitutes the basis, or heart, of the system.

The purpose of the exposition heretofore has been to construct the fundamental shape of a strictly legal comprehension of law. I have designated this approach strictly legal because of Hart's stated intention to look at law in its distinctiveness, in its isolation from other contexts. I would contend that Hart's concept of law is both intelligible and useful. It provides categories and distinctions that can be employed in the analysis and interpretation of legal phenomena. But it is a limited construction, the limitations deriving from its perspective and its narrowly defined context. In the next section we move to another context and, consequently, another level of comprehension.

Social Context

Lon Luvois Fuller and H. L. A. Hart have been locked in a jurisprudential battle of about ten years' standing. In part the battle is a result of differing perspectives. Hart views law from a strictly legal perspective; Fuller sees law within the context of social purposes. When understood in this manner, the two positions, at least as I shall exploit them in this exposition, are not incompatible. A point of contact is derivable from Fuller's latest book, *The Morality of Law* (1964), in which, as a formal definition, law is conceived as "the enterprise of subjecting human conduct to the governance of rules."[15] There is a difference, however, in point of concentration. To exaggerate the difference, I shall construe Harold J. Berman as representing Fuller's position where he declaims that "law is not *essentially* a body of rules at all" but rather "an institution in the sense of an integrated pattern or process of social behavior and ideas."[16]

According to Fuller, man is, among other things, a purposive, creative, deciding projective being. This self-determinative character carries over from man as an individual to man in society. Organizations and institutions are basically expressions of human purposiveness. Associations are not merely patterns of interaction; more profoundly, they are structures of expectation and purposive reaching. It is within this context that Fuller's notions of the internal morality of law and the external morality of law are properly understood.[17]

All social processes entail a form of internal or inner morality, however simple or short range it might be. Chester I. Barnard's *The Functions of the Executive*[18] is cited by Fuller as illustrative of this proposition. In that book Barnard explores the rules of human conduct that inhere in the attempt to create and maintain formal organization, particularly in the area of business administration. A formal organization is a structured process; it involves multiple actions and continuous decision making; it is, so to say, always becoming. Seriously to purpose a formal organization requires commitment to a host of detailed requisites. In other words, a collection of people may project as a dominant aim the formation and maintenance of an organization, but the satisfactory fulfilment of that dominant aim entails sustained conformity of action to all the norms that constitute the full meaning of that aim. What is true of formal business organization is true of any modality of human association, if not indeed of any sequence of purposive behavior. To cast this concept in more formal terms, if a person or a group of people seriously project purpose x, then they are obliged to conform in their decisions and actions to norms $x_1, x_2, x_3, \ldots n$, which are implied in the actualization of x. The implied norms in any particular form of social order constitute what Fuller designates its "internal morality." At times he has characterized this level of norms as "procedural natural law" in the sense that it consists of principles of action that inhere in the nature of the particular form of social process under examination. I would suggest that the term "contingent morality" might also be employed in order to convey the conditional character of this level of norms. Its operativeness depends upon continued commitment to the dominant purpose. The abandonment or discontinuance of the overriding project dissolves the obligation to conform to the procedural norms.

In Fuller's conception, law is a form of social process; it is a cooperative enterprise; it is a goal or aim or purpose of a group of persons. Precisely, it is the purpose of subjecting human conduct to the governance of rules. But like many other social purposes, this cannot be once accomplished and then forgotten. It requires persistent activity by many people for as long as the purpose is alive. The realization of the purpose bears with it the norms of the "internal morality of law," or what is called variously "the special morality of law," "the procedural natural law of law," "the principles of legality," and "legal morality."

Fuller identifies eight principles or qualities or "kinds of legal excellence." If there is a total lack of conformity to any one of these principles, then the purposive enterprise of law collapses. The creation and continuance of law are contingent upon adherence to all of these principles at least to some degree. The principles, cast in negative form, are these:

1. The principle of generality: law cannot exist where decisions are completely ad hoc.
2. The principle of promulgation: law cannot exist where all rules are kept secret.
3. The principle of prospectiveness: law cannot exist where all rules are retrospective.
4. The principle of clarity: law cannot exist where rules are totally unintelligible.
5. The principle of consistency: law cannot exist where the rules are incompatible with each other.
6. The principle of possibility: law cannot exist where the rules demand what is impossible.
7. The principle of stability: law cannot exist where the rules are altered at every moment.
8. The principle of congruence: law cannot exist where the rules

administered by officials are completely incongruent with the rules promulgated.

There are instances when it is permissible and even important to violate these principles. They are more generally regulative than absolutely necessary norms. Moreover, when the norms are applied in some concrete situation, they may clash, and the determination of which shall prevail depends upon prudential decision. Further, it is possible that additional rules are formulable and that a recombination or restatement of these principles might prove more fruitful. But a legal system cannot exist without some degree of conformity to these norms of the internal morality of law.

In this connection, Fuller, like Hart, argues that legal systems do not merely exist or not exist. There are degrees of existence, perhaps even degrees of health, assessable by employing the eight principles as categories of analysis. This means that the eight principles of the internal morality of law can function both as a means of interpretation and, in perhaps two senses, for purposes of evaluation. On the one hand, the *legal analyst* can use them as a measure of the relative success or health of a legal system. On the other hand, the *participant in a legal order* can use them as a measure for criticism, as a guideline for the formulation of policies for improvement, and as an instrument in considering the question of legal obligation. It will be recalled that, according to *Hart's* concept of law, obligatoriness is an intrinsic aspect of law as such. Once a rule is adjudged as valid by reference to the rule of recognition, it is a matter of obligation, although, to be sure, the fact of validity is not ipso facto determinative of acceptance or even obedience. On the other hand, according to *Fuller's* concept of law, beyond the question of the validity of a particular rule lies the question of the legality of the system. A high degree of capriciousness, secrecy, inconsistency, vagueness, incongruence, etc., in the actual operation of what purports to be a legal system may justify resistance or even opposition to it because it is insufficiently law to warrant acceptance, the relative validity of the rules notwithstanding. Admittedly, actual circumstances seldom permit a clean-cut judgment; a decision of non-obligation invariably involves a degree of arbitrariness; levels of tolerability vary, and other factors properly enter such a serious decision. But the eight principles provide one with some rational basis for decision, and the basis is not extraneous to law. Rather, it is an intrinsic aspect of law itself, when law is viewed as a social process whose purpose is the subjection of human conduct to the governance of rules.

In a critical comment on Fuller's notion of the internal morality of law, Hart asks why the term "morality" should be employed, since in fact the eight qualities are but principles of good craftsmanship, much like the principles of the poisoner's art. Hart's contention is that adherence to the qualities of legality does not in itself guarantee that the legal system as a whole or some aspect of it will not be immoral, or directed to morally evil ends. That contention is undeniable, and Fuller does not deny it. But as far as morality includes rules of obligation and as far as the eight principles constitute obligations given commitment to the purpose of law, then clearly the term morality is appropriate. And as far as what purports to be a legal system possesses the qualities of legality, it may be properly considered "good" to that extent and on that level. But evaluative judgments of a legal system derive from other levels as well, which levels provide additional dimensions to the understanding of the nature of law.

One of these other levels involves at least part of what Fuller means by "the external morality of law."

As we have observed, societies, using the term here in a generic sense, are expressions of human purpose. In *The Problems of Jurisprudence* (1949),[19] Fuller employs the term "common need" to designate the purposiveness that underlies, informs, and in an important way constitutes a society.[20]

In a relatively simple society, the members may all understand the common need and work toward its actualization without serious disagreement and perhaps even without deliberation. But in practically all societies, particularly large, complicated, political societies, the common need—the structure of expectation and purpose—is not so unmixed, homogeneous, and obvious. The social purpose may contain antagonistic aspects; individual need may conflict with societal aim; persons and associations within the society may disagree radically as to the essential components of the common need and the most expeditious way of fulfilling the need; there may even be contention over how to resolve matters of contention; the content of common need and social purpose may shift and change over the course of time; and there seems to be no sure and certain method of testing any particular formulation of the social purpose of a society at any given time.

But, despite these complexities and difficulties, Fuller insists— on the basis of the premises that human action is purposive and that associations are created, maintained, transformed, and destroyed by human action—that a common set of purposes constitutes the foundation of a society. The common set of purposes of a society is in large part what Fuller refers to as the external morality of law.

That is, to Fuller, law is itself a social process, but only as an aspect of a more inclusive social process; law is itself a purposive enterprise, but only as an aspect of a more inclusive purposive enterprise. It is possible and it may be helpful to view and to analyze law abstractly, in formal terms, in strictly legal terms; but law is always operative within the context of a social-political reality. A legal system is a more or less differentiable dimension of that reality whose driving force is a more or less integrated complex of purposes, goals, expectations, and interests. This complex social purpose is among the determinative criteria for assessing alternative answers to questions concerning law—whether a legal system is desirable, what its content and aims should be, what its proper limitations are, whether its effects are what was intended, if it should be altered in procedural form or in substantive ingredients. In this sense it is tempting to say that society controls or ought to control law, but that proposition is a confusing oversimplification, for there is no clear boundary separating society and law. Law is not merely a tool of society in the sense in which a hoe is a tool for a gardener. Rather, the legal system is the society itself in one of its modes of interaction. Thus the assessment and evaluation of the legal process from the standpoint of social purpose occurs partially within the legal process itself, and the legal process may even contribute to the formulation and reformulation of the purposes of the more inclusive body.

This understanding of law as located within the context of society bears on the question of the grounds of acceptance. Without neglecting the actual intricacy of the relation between law and society, one may posit the analytic extremes of disjunction and conformity. Disjunction means that the effect of a legal system is totally inconsistent with the purposive pattern of all other aspects of the social process; in such a situation, acceptance is unlikely. Conformity means that the effect of a legal system is in all respects consistent with the purposive pattern of the inclusive society; in that situation, acceptance is probably assured. In between the two extremes, the degree of acceptance probably depends on a number of variables, but surely one of the most crucial is the relative compatibility of the legal system's effect and the projected purposes of the society.[21] The secondary rules of a legal system must be to some degree accepted if the system is to be effective. But to be accepted at all, the system in procedure and in effect must be to some extent responsive to the social forces that create and maintain it. Abuse is, of course, possible; the system can operate somewhat on the basis of sheer obedience; but there are limits of tolerability, and even before the limits of tolerability are reached, the bounds of acceptance have been transgressed, at which moment law no longer functions as law.

This is another way of saying that the morality of a society, in the sense of the goals, purposes, interests, and aims of the people, plays a crucial—perhaps essential—role in the formation and maintenance of law, at least at the vital point of acceptance. Hart does not completely deny this, as evidenced in his affirmation:

> What surely is most needed in order to make men clear sighted in confronting the official abuse of power, is that they should preserve the sense that the certification of something as legally valid is not conclusive of the question of obedience [and a fortiori the question of acceptance?], and that, however great the aura of majesty or authority which the official system may have, its demands must in the end be subjected to a moral scrutiny.[22]

More importantly, he asserts that a legal system is most stable and most healthy when its acceptance rests on a sense of moral obligation. *However,* he insists, with good reason, that the range of possible motivations leading to acceptance embraces non- and extramoral considerations as well. That is the basis on which Hart denies a necessary connection between law and morality. Nonetheless, contra Hart, it is difficult to conceive of a legal system existing without *some* proportion of the people affected accepting the system or some significant aspect of the system as morally good from *some* perspective, even if the only principle invoked is the principle of the lesser evil. This judgment must not be construed as meaning that all law is per se morally good from whatever perspective. What it does mean is that law is imbedded within and is itself an aspect of a more inclusive social process, and as such it is subject to an "external morality"; its existence is, in the strict sense, a precarious one, depending upon conformity to that morality.[23]

Thus the comprehension of law within its social context draws attention to dimensions of understanding that tend to be subdued or neglected altogether when the context is limited to the strictly legal. The notion of the internal morality of law which derives from viewing law as itself a social process adds meaning to the concept of law as the explicit attempt to subject human conduct to the governance of rules; the notion of the external morality of law which derives from viewing law as an aspect within a more inclusive social process adds meaning to the concept of acceptance and therefore to the general dynamics and destiny of legal processes. Altogether, this comprehension of law contributes categories and distinctions, however general, that can be fruitfully exploited in analyzing, interpreting, and even evaluating law. However, there is another context that provides a further dimension to the understanding of law.

Religious-Humanistic Context

The third context that constitutes a basis for a perspective on law is the religious-humanistic. The relation between religion and humanism is perhaps not immediately evident, for much depends on what exactly religion and humanism are understood to mean.

Without taking this as an exhaustive definition, Max Weber has suggested that "Religion claims to offer an ultimate stand toward the world by virtue of a direct grasp of the world's 'meaning,'" and, again, "all religions have demanded as a specific presupposition that the course of the world be somehow *meaningful,* at least so far as it touches upon the interests of men."[24] Somewhat more narrowly but not inconsistently, it might be fruitful to render religion as interest in and concern for salvation. To do so, of course, requires an attempt to divest the term "salvation" of merely particular significance, limited, say, to flight into the ethereal realm while cloaked in garments of pure white. Salvation, in general terms, involves notions of ultimate destiny and instant condition, of final end and immediate situation. In the words of Josiah Royce, there are two member elements contained in the concept of salvation.

> The first is the idea that there is some end or aim of human life which is more important than all other aims, so that, by comparison with this aim all else is secondary and subsidiary, and perhaps relatively unimportant, or even vain and empty. The other idea is this: That man as he now is, or as he naturally is, is in great danger of so missing this highest aim as to render his whole life a senseless failure by virtue of this coming short of his true good.[25]

This construction of religion as concern for salvation is not absent from the formulations of religion as "a framework of orientation and devotion" (Erich Fromm), "ultimate concern" (Paul Tillich) and of religious faith as "the attitude and action of confidence in, and fidelity to, certain realities as the sources of value and objects of loyalty" (H. R. Niebuhr). In each of these capsule definitions, there is reference, directly or indirectly, to an object that is of final importance for human existence—an object of devotion, a matter of ultimate concern, a reality that constitutes the source of value and object of loyalty. Man's relation to that object provides him with a sense of the meaning of the world, constitutes the fundamental basis of normative judgments and behavioral patterns, and furnishes an earnest and at least fragmentary actualization of fulfilment (salvation).

There is a manifest point of contact between this comprehensive understanding of religion and Fuller's premise concerning man and society as inherently and inescapably purposive, for from a religious perspective as well, man is a purposive being, properly oriented toward an ultimate destiny, a final good, an absolute value. And this is or may be true both of individual persons and collectivities. It has been widely proposed that there exists no person or society without religious faith of some character. As far as this is the case, the structure of purposes that constitutes the foundation of a society is religious at its core. This is perhaps what Augustine meant in his definition of a people as "an assemblage of reasonable beings bound together by a common agreement as to the objects of their love."[26] A society is what it loves. Love here means the fundamental orientation of persons toward something that is apprehended as of ultimate value. On this basis, Paul Tillich constructed his analysis of the spirit of capitalist society in *The Religious Situation,* demonstrating the manner in which a particular ultimate attitude permeates, qualifies, informs the scientific, artistic, political, ecclesiastical, and moral activities of the culture.[27] Likewise, on this basis, H. Richard Niebuhr explored the multiple forms of religious faith that play throughout the various areas and dimensions of Western civilization.[28]

The understanding of religion presented to this point implies that there is a more or less direct connection between a people's religion and a people's law. In simplest form (but only in simplest form), if law is an aspect of a more inclusive social process, and if the fundamental identity of that social process is the ultimate purposiveness that is religious in character, then the legal system will undoubtedly be informed by religion. In other words, religion is the cardinal level and creative source of the external morality of law. A particular faith, however widely or narrowly shared, provides the ultimate context for the analysis, interpretation, and evaluation of all other dimensions of the *external morality of law,* of the condition of the legal process with reference to the *internal morality of law,* and of the content and operation of both the *primary and secondary rules of the legal system.* This concept of religion and of its relevance to the understanding of law is of a generic character. On the more specific level, at the heart of Christianity, following Judaism, is the proclamation that the true God, the true object of religious faith, is he whose creative and redemptive work in the world is characterized most specifically as love. Love is, in this connection, the drive toward the actualization of universal community in which the individuality of each is qualified by a concern for all. Community is "the order in which the members of a society are so related that the freedom, uniqueness, and power of each serves the freedom, uniqueness and growth of all the other members."[29] Within the actual passage of history, the community of all with all is both received and repulsed, both realized and confounded. Meaning, from this perspective, derives from apprehending the actual occasions of human interaction in relation to the intentional workings of the God of love. And the fundamental imperative and final purpose of a man's existence is to participate in the divine process, shattering its obstructions and actualizing its possibilities in both individual and social form.

Christian faith as here represented is a form of humanism, for the central thrust of the divine process is understood to be the fulfilment or salvation of mankind—the humanization of man. To the extent to which the formation of community is thwarted and opposed, man's own nature is violated; to the extent to which any man's unique individuality and creative activity are crushed, his being as a man is denied; to the extent to which, in the arrangements of human existence, certain groups of persons are arbitrarily denied access to the value of civilization and society, the fulfilment of man's humanity is compromised.

Something of this character of thinking resides at the basis of natural law theory of law.[30] Relative to this point, there is a dimension of Lon Fuller's jurisprudence that bears examination. In a few scattered places in his writings on legal theory, Fuller has postulated three norms of law conceived as universally applicable because they concern the preservation of man's humanity. In 1954, while professing ignorance of any absolute moral norm that would yield clear directives for decision in all circumstances, he nonetheless declared that "human life is . . . as close to an absolute as anything we have."[31] In 1955, he asserted that the one general social objective without which all others lose their meaning is "the objective of keeping alive the creative, choosing, purposive side of man's nature."[32] And in 1964, he wrote, "If I were asked . . . to discern one central indisputable principle of what may be called substantive natural law . . . I would find it in the injunction: Open up, maintain, and preserve the

integrity of the channels of communication by which men convey to
one another what they perceive, feel, and desire."[33] To Fuller, human
persons are intrinsically living, purposing, communicating beings.
To act in such a way as to crush life, to thwart purposiveness, or to
obstruct communication is to deny the humanity of the persons affected. Fuller is abundantly aware of the tragic character of history
and of the necessity of compromise given the circumstantial limitations of action. But, with all that, he posits as the ultimate directive
or rule of human action—individual and social—the trilogic norm:
preserve human life, keep alive the purposive side of man's nature,
maintain communication. Fuller does not press his analysis into the
religious dimension; there is good reason to suppose that, with Max
Weber, he is by open profession "religiously unmusical," though not
religiously unsympathetic. But surely these three norms are compat-
ible with the notion of community as explicated; indeed, on the basis
of the understanding of religion presented in the first portion of this
section, it may not be farfetched to argue that Fuller is not without
religious faith in fact and these three fundamental norms are expression of his implicit religiousness, which possesses a Judaic-Christian
character.

Even if that final argument involves a definitional sleight of hand,
it is still possible to appropriate Fuller's trilogic norm as an extension
or implicate of the Judaic-Christian notions of love and community.
Relative to legal theory, the significance of this connection is found
in the fact that it is out of this norm that Fuller has developed his
concept of the "rule of law." "The essence of the rule of law," he
writes, "lies in the fact that men affected by the decisions which
emerge from social processes should have some formally guaranteed
opportunity to affect those decisions."[34] There are a number of social
processes by which the rule of law may be affected—elective procedures, contractual possibilities, institutions for adjudication, etc. Exactly which process is desirable depends on the type of decision. But
whatever the institutional process, the crucial consideration is to
keep open lines of communication and thus to keep alive the purposive aspect of human nature on the part of all persons affected by
resultant decisions.

Thus out of the particular form of religious-humanistic context
exhibited here as Judaic-Christian, law is comprehended as a principle of human decision making. To the extent to which any purported
legal system fails to conform to that principle, it is unacceptable; and,
even within Hart's strictly legal context, without acceptance law does

not function as law. In the assessment of an alleged legal system by the rule of law, the procedural aspects of law are of prime importance, for the procedures are not mere technicalities; they are constituents of the quality of human action and interaction; they are patterns or modes of relationship. As such, they may be more or less expressive of community, which is both the divine intent for man and the specifically human destiny of man. From this perspective, the question to raise particularly of the secondary rules of a system—rules of recognition, change, and adjudication—concerns in what way and how effectively they permit participation in their operation, in what way and how effectively they keep open the possibility of communication, in what way and how effectively they maintain respect for human persons as human persons.

Having come to this point, I do not mean to contend that of the three contexts—the strictly legal, the social, and the religious-humanistic—in which law may be observed, one is correct, valid, true, and proper, and the other two are not. But I do mean to contend that each of the perspectives provides an orientation and a set of categories that are useful in the understanding of law. Moreover, I mean to contend that a sufficient comprehension of law requires attention to all three levels, for all are aspects of the total reality within which law operates. Law is a set of rules, but even as a set of rules it depends for its efficacy upon acceptance, and acceptance depends upon its effect on and reception by the people affected. Law is a social process, but even as a social process it has impact upon the condition of people as human beings; it contributes to or detracts from the full actualization of man's humanity. Law is a human enterprise, but even as such it is a dimension of the divine-human encounter on which the salvation of man depends. In sum, this statement may be conceived as a programmatic sketch in legal theory, indicating a mode of reconciling three diverse forms of jurisprudential thought—analytic, sociological, and natural law—in such a way that the genius of each is preserved, the connection with the others is demonstrated, and their relation to religious thought is explained.

Applicability

The adequacy of legal theory depends at least in part upon applicability in legal analysis and legal practice. Consequently, in this last section of this paper I shall illustrate the usefulness of the contexts and categories that appear in the preceding sections. First, I shall present a series of comments on the recent Supreme Court case

Miranda v. *Arizona* (1966);[35] second and briefly, I shall present an observation on legal education.

By way of general description, *Miranda* v. *Arizona* is the most recent of a sequence of Supreme Court decisions dealing with criminal procedural law. This decision bears on the manner in which and the extent to which the Fifth Amendment privilege against self-incrimination and the Sixth Amendment right to counsel are to be effected. Further extending a line ranging from *Powell* (1932)[36] through *Gideon* (1963)[37] and *Escobedo* (1964),[38] *Miranda* provides that in all instances, federal and state, of felonies and (perhaps) misdemeanors, once a suspect's freedom of action is curtailed in any way by police, he must be clearly apprised of his constitutional rights and privileges. The majority opinion, written by Chief Justice Earl Warren, sets forth "constitutional guidelines" detailing procedures police must employ to assure the protection of the accused. A person under custody must be informed in unequivocal terms (1) that he has the right to remain silent, (2) that anything he says may be used against him in court, (3) that he has right to counsel at that point and throughout any interrogation of him, and (4) that if he is indigent he has the right to have counsel appointed to represent him, paid out of public funds. Moreover, if the suspect has been so informed but has waived these rights, and if the prosecutor uses what is said in court, the burden of proof is upon the prosecutor to demonstrate that the suspect was informed, understood the issue, knowingly waived his rights, and agreed to make a statement. Without proof of that sort, the results of interrogation are not admissible as evidence. The opinion carefully emphasizes that Congress or the states may develop alternative procedures to secure the privileges of the accused, on the stipulation that they be as fully effective as those outlined. Meanwhile, these "constitutional guidelines" are, for all effects and purposes, legal rules.

1. Within the strictly legal context, *Miranda* illustrates (*a*) the complexity of the rule of recognition in the American legal system, (*b*) the interplay among secondary rules, (*c*) the possibility of reluctant acceptance, and (*d*) indirectly something of the character of the primary rules of the system.

(*a*) The complexity and the open texture of the rule of recognition in the American legal system are evidenced in most if not all constitutional law cases in the sense that, on the one hand, the validity of the Supreme Court rests upon the Constitution; but, on the other hand, the Constitution is, in important ways, created by the Supreme

Court. This dialectical character of the rule of recognition is implicitly acknowledged in both the majority and the dissenting opinions of *Miranda*. The majority opinion claims to be only applying the law as found in the Constitution, yet admits the relative novelty of the instant decision. Harlan's dissent concludes with the bitter statement, "Nothing in the letter or spirit of the Constitution or in the precedents squares with the heavy-handed and one-sided action that is so precipitously taken by the Court in the name of fulfilling its constitutional responsibilities"—whereby Harlan both demonstrates acceptance of the Constitution (and precedents) as the fundamental rule of recognition, yet reluctantly admits that what the Court has decided is valid. The same observation can be made of White's dissenting assertion that the constitutional right against self-incrimination cannot be construed, by a reading of the text, to apply to such an early stage in the investigatory process—but it surely applies to that stage now.

(*b*) There is an interplay between rule of recognition and rule of adjudication in the *Miranda* case, illustrating the supremacy of the rule of recognition over the other secondary rules of a system. The constitutional guidelines enacted by the Court are, in effect, legal directives shaping the initial stages of the adjudicatory process, for the precise question with which the police are concerned when apprehending a suspect is whether on a given occasion the primary rules of obligation have been broken.

(*c*) Reluctant acceptance is represented, not only in the dissenting opinions as observed above, but also in numerous other reactions to the decision. New York City's Police Commissioner Howard R. Leary, after a gibe about developing sophisticated law in an immature society and a prediction about diminishing law and order, nonetheless said, "You have the law of the land and you have to obey it."[39]

(*d*) The *Miranda* case might be construed to bear distantly and indirectly upon the primary rules of obligation. Admittedly, the subject of the decision is procedural law, and therefore it does not direct or empower citizens to act or to refrain from acting in certain ways in relation to each other. But the rights that are filled out in *Miranda* are expressions of a general legal direction in American society to establish limits to the extent of governmental power, to provide the individual person with legally guaranteed actions and movements. The *Miranda* case, within context, has the connotation of favoring a certain type of social order, labeled "libertarian" by one commentator.[40]

2. Within the social context, *Miranda* manifests the operation of both the internal and the external morality of law.

(*a*) There are three principles of the internal morality of law evident in the case. First, the Supreme Court in this decision was attending to the principle of clarity. In the sequence of preceding cases, a number of points were unclear. At what point in the investigatory proceedings does a suspect have the right to counsel and the right to remain silent? Must police inform him of his rights and, if so, when? At what point in the proceedings are indigents entitled to counsel? By what test is a court to ascertain whether a confession has been coerced? Do the same rules in these matters apply throughout the entire system?

The unclarity in this area of criminal law was attested to by the fact that both the American Law Institute and the President's Commission on Law Enforcement and Administration of Justice had been drafting model codes to answer some of these questions. Chief Justice Warren, in the opinion, took account of these problems and announced that the guidelines were designed exactly to provide a clear rule.

Second, on the basis of the contention that a significant proportion of persons apprehended by the police have been unaware of precisely what their legal rights and privileges were, this Supreme Court decision helps to overcome a deficiency in promulgation.

Third, the *Miranda* case should increase the degree of adherence to the principle of congruence between declared rule and official action, for, assuming that police will conform with the guidelines, greater effect will be given to the constitutional guarantees of the Bill of Rights.

(*b*) The external morality of law refers to questions of social purposes, goals, values, interests. Such questions almost invariably lurk in the background of Supreme Court cases, which is the reason why these cases are so often controversial. As Robert G. McCloskey has observed, "they pit one set of crucial values against another in a near balance, and the criminal procedure cases illustrate this nicely."[41]

On the surface, the stated values that have come to the fore in the *Miranda* case are (1) the suppression of crime by swift and effective means, since crime is disruptive of the social order; and (2) the protection of persons against physical and psychological coercion in the solicitation of information concerning apparent criminal activity, since such coercion may lead to the punishment of innocent parties. Some persons concerned with (1) have predicted an appreciable increase in crime and an increased threat to the security of private citizens as a result of the new decision and have therefore advocated amendment of the Constitution to nullify *Miranda*. On the other hand, some persons concerned with (2) challenge the predictions and insist that law enforcement will not or at least need not be affected— but even if it is, the constitutional rights are too precious to erode.[42]

3. Within the religious-humanistic context, there are two observations to make.

(*a*) The religious context is in part an extension of the social context. This is to say that the needs and interests that are expressed through the interpretation and critique of law express one's underlying religiousness. But how to divine the exact character of that latter dimension through participation in and reaction to legal matters is a major problem of hermeneutics. The following two comments are merely attempts to hazard a guess of the religious direction of response to *Miranda*. To overdraw the case, those who support at least the spirit of the *Miranda* decision tend to stand in the libertarian tradition exemplified historically in the emergence of free-enterprise capitalism and in Jeffersonianism and more recently in movements to effectuate locally and universally the kinds of principles expressed in the Universal Declaration of the Rights of Man. Such persons are willing to take the risks and pay the costs of maintaining and extending legal principles that are productive of a free and open society. It would be unfair to say that those who stand opposed to *Miranda* (even though they accept it as law) are enemies of a free society and opposed to the rights of individuals. But, aside from the difficult question of the relative accuracy or inaccuracy of statistics and predictions about crime that are used to shore up the dissenting side, it might be fair to ascribe to them a weighty concern for security, for orderliness, for authoritative, firm, close control over the members of society—a concern sufficient to warrant a recommendation that the constitution be amended and the legal-social order changed, however slightly.

(*b*) With a slight touch of audacity, I suggest that the *Miranda* decision, in its general intent if not in its specific detail, may be viewed approvingly from the Judaic-Christian-humanistic position. At the point that a suspect is taken into police custody, an important decision-making process has been initiated. It is only proper, according to the rule of law, that the suspect be informed about the implications of the interchange and be given expert advice so that he may remain informed and assisted throughout the process. Moreover, the full social effect of the guidelines in *Miranda* is to equalize the treatment of persons who become implicated in the enforcement and investigatory procedure, for it appears that under previously prevailing police practice, the poor, the uneducated, and the minority-group member were the ones deprived of their privileges. While there is no legal method of assuring the full actualization of community, there are legal methods of overcoming its most flagrant obstacles, and *Miranda* is a means of assisting that cause.

I conclude with a brief comment on legal education. If primary attention is devoted to the strictly legal understanding of law, then the prevailing method of legal education is appropriate. The case law method taught in the tradition of Langdell and Ames is the rule in America. And it is intelligible both as providing training in an intriguing form of reasoning and as preparing jurists for the technical aspect of their profession. Certainly without an intimate acquaintance with the body of highly specialized legal materials and without the skill to conduct legal research, a jurist would be unable to fulfil his professional responsibilities.

But the legal profession exists within a social context. Many persons trained in law fulfil other than strictly legal roles in the social order, and even those who do are in an enterprise that has a wide and important social impact. This is why McDougal and Lasswell two decades ago proposed the complete transformation of legal education around the conception of law as a policy science oriented toward "the ever more complete achievement of the democratic values that constitute the professed ends of American policy."[43] Something of this same approach underlies the majestic (but still only privately published) manuscript of Henry Hart and Albert Sacks, *The Legal Process,* in which they attempt to conceive law as purposive in character, providing directive arrangements within a more general social process.[44]

Probably in most law schools the religious perspective is completely ignored as far as deliberate attention is concerned. That does not make it less operative. What perhaps can and should be proposed are greater explicit concern for the actual effect of law upon men and women as human persons and more express consideration of the implications of the rule of law throughout the various areas of legal practice. This proposal derives from the contention that law, beyond its strictly legal and social contexts, resides within a human-divine context, and is only fully and adequately comprehended when it is understood in that light.

NOTES

1. Alan Gewirth, "The Quest for Specificity in Jurisprudence," *Ethics* 69 (1959) 155.

2. H. L. A. Hart, *The Concept of Law* (London: Oxford University Press, 1961).

3. The continued value of Hart's book is attested to by the fact that in 1966 the faculty of the Harvard Law School awarded its distinguished James Barr Ames Prize for outstanding legal scholarship to Hart because of the book.

4. It is instructive to note that Hart often qualifies the noun "rule" with the adjective "social."

5. "The living law is the law which dominates life itself even though it has not been posited in legal propositions" (Eugen Ehrlich, *The Fundamental Principles of the Sociology of Law* [trans. Walter L. Moll; New York: Russell & Russell, 1962] 493).

6. Hart, *The Concept of Law,* 41.

7. Ibid., 91.

8. Clifford Pannam, "Professor Hart and Analytical Jurisprudence," *Journal of Legal Education* 16 (1964) 397.

9. Hart, *The Concept of Law, 88.*

10. Ibid.

11. Ibid., 113.

12. I have constructed a table (shown below) to summarize the major considerations in Hart's concept of law (as analyzed to this point) in ascertaining the relative *status of a legal system.*

	Response of citizens to primary legal rules	*Response of officials to secondary legal rules*
1. HEALTHY	Complete acceptance	Complete acceptance
2. EXISTENT	Proportional acceptance	
	Obedience without acceptance	Proportional acceptance
3. PATHOLOGICAL	Proportional disobedience	
		Complete non-acceptance
4. NON-EXISTENT	Complete disobedience	

13. Hart, *The Concept of Law,* 109.

14. Ibid., 115.

15. Lon L. Fuller, *The Morality of Law* (New Haven and London: Yale University Press, 1964) 96, 106, 146.

16. Harold J. Berman, *The Nature and Functions of Law* (Brooklyn, N.Y.: Foundation Press, 1958) 8, 9. Italics in the original.

17. For a systematic exposition of Lon Fuller's basis [*sic*] jurisprudential thought, see my article, "Lon Fuller's Multidimensional Natural Law Theory," *Stanford Law Review* 18 (1966) 612–39.

18. Chester I. Barnard, *The Functions of the Executive* (Cambridge, Mass.: Harvard University Press, 1945).

19. Lon L. Fuller, *The Problems of Jurisprudence* (temporary ed.; Brooklyn, N.Y.: Foundation Press, 1949) 694–701.

20. Fuller is vulnerable to the charge that he underplays, even almost completely ignores, the unconscious, customary, traditional, organic dimensions of social process, which oversight may derive from the fact that, besides jurisprudence, one of his areas of specialization is contract law. Granting the overbalance, it is nonetheless illuminating to view social process in its more purposive, future-oriented aspect.

21. I suspect that this is the train of thought that underlies Fuller's recent tendency to emphasize the category of reciprocity in human relationships. See Lon L. Fuller, "Irrigation and Tyranny," *Stanford Law Review* 17 (1965) 1027–30.

22. Hart, *The Concept of Law,* 206.

23. As an incidental observation, I suggest that the relative difference between Hart and Fuller on this subject is founded in part on the fact that Hart tends (not without qualification) to restrict morality to *Gesinnungsethik,* to deontological ethics, in his explicit comments about morality in *The Concept of Law,* whereas Fuller tends (again, not without qualification) to use the term "morality" in the sense of *Verantwortungsethik,* of a mode of teleological ethics, when reflecting constructively about the relation between law and morality. The full complexity of their uses of the term "morality" remains to be explored.

24. *From Max Weber: Essays in Sociology* (ed. and trans. H. H. Gerth and C. Wright Mills; London: Routledge & Kegan Paul, 1952) 352ff. Italics in the original.

25. Josiah Royce, *The Sources of Religious Insight* (New York: Charles Scribner's Sons, 1940) 12. Italics removed.

26. Augustine *Civitate Dei* 19.24.

27. Paul Tillich, *The Religious Situation* (trans. H. Richard Niebuhr; New York: Meridian Books, 1956).

28. H. Richard Niebuhr, *Radical Monotheism and Western Culture* (New York: Harper & Row, 1960).

29. Daniel Day Williams, *God's Grace and Man's Hope* (New York: Harper & Bros., 1949) 151.

30. See my article "Naturalism, Historicism, and Christian Ethics: Toward a Christian Doctrine of Natural Law," *Journal of Religion* 44 (1964) 40–51. This was republished in *New Theology No. 2* (ed. Martin E. Marty and Dean G. Peerman; New York: Macmillan Co., 1965) 77–96.

31. Lon L. Fuller, "American Legal Philosophy at Mid-Century," *Journal of Legal Education* 6 (1954) 467.

32. Lon L. Fuller, "Freedom—A Suggested Analysis," *Harvard Law Review* 68 (1955) 1314.

33. Fuller, *The Morality of Law,* 186.

34. Lon L. Fuller, "Collective Bargaining and the Arbitrator," *Wisconsin Law Review* 1 (1963) 19. See also Lon L. Fuller, "Adjudication and the Rule of Law," *Proceedings of the American Society of International Law* (1960) 2.

35. 384 U.S. 436.

36. *Powell* v. *Alabama,* 287 U.S. 45, 53 S. Ct. 55 (1932).

37. *Gideon* v. *Wainwright,* 372 U.S. 335, 83 S. Ct. 792 (1963).

38. *Escobedo* v. *Illinois,* 378 U.S. 478, 84 S. Ct. 1758 (1964).

39. Quoted in the *New York Times,* 15 June 1966, p. 28.

40. Sidney E. Zion, "Beyond Escobedo Case," *New York Times,* 14 June 1966, p. 25.

41. Robert G. McCloskey, ed., *Essays in Constitutional Law* (New York: Random House, 1957) 382.

42. It is intriguing to note Roscoe Pound's vigorous defense of position (1) on presumed socio-historical grounds as early as 1921 in his *The Spirit of the Common Law* (Boston: Beacon Press, 1963) 103–6.

43. Harold D. Lasswell and Myres S. McDougal, "Legal Education and Public Policy: Professional Training in the Public Interest," in Harold D. Lasswell, *The Analysis of Political Behavior: An Empirical Approach* (New York: Oxford University Press, 1949) 24.

44. Henry M. Hart, Jr., and Albert M. Sacks, *The Legal Process: Basic Problems in the Making and Application of Law* (Cambridge, Mass., 1958).

PART THREE

MORAL OBJECTIONS
TO LAW

7

The Obligation to
Disobey the Law*

Michael Walzer

The Obligation to Disobey

According to liberal political theory, as formulated by John Locke, any individual citizen, oppressed by the rulers of the state, has a right to disobey their commands, break their laws, even rebel and seek to replace the rulers and change the laws. In fact, however, this is not a right often claimed or acted upon by individuals. Throughout history, when men have disobeyed or rebelled, they have done so, by and large, as members or representatives of groups, and they have claimed, not merely that they are free to disobey, but that they are obligated to do so. Locke says nothing about such obligations, and, despite the fact that Thomas Jefferson claimed on behalf of the American colonists that "it is their right, it is their duty, to throw off [despotism]," the idea that men can be obligated to disobey has not played much part in liberal political theory.

"Here I stand; I can do no other"—Martin Luther's bold defiance—is hardly an assertion of freedom or a claim to rights. It is the acknowledgment of a new but undeniable obligation. Nor is this obligation often asserted, as it was by Luther, in the first-person singular. In a recent article on civil disobedience, Hugo Bedau has denied the validity of such an assertion, unless it is supplemented by arguments which reach beyond the moral feelings of the individual. "The force

---

*First published in *Political Theory and Social Change* (ed. David Spitz; 1967) 187–202; republished in *Ethics* 77 (1967) 163–75 and in *Obligations: Essays on Disobedience, War, and Citizenship* by Michael Walzer (1970) 3–23.

of saying, 'I ought to disobey this law' cannot be derived from 'Obeying this law is inconsistent with my moral convictions.'"[1] Perhaps it cannot, and then we must wait upon Luther's further defense before we judge his defiance. But the first sentence is, in practice, rarely derived from the second. Generally it follows from an assertion of a very different sort: "Obeying this law is inconsistent with *our* moral convictions (on behalf of which we have made significant commitments, organized, worked together for so many months or years, and so on)." And it can be argued that, having said this, one can then go on, without offering additional reasons, to say, "Therefore I ought to disobey." This, at any rate, is the form that disobedience most often takes in history, even though additional reasons are usually offered. Men rarely break the law by themselves, or if they do they rarely talk about it. Disobedience, when it is not criminally but morally, religiously, or politically motivated, is almost always a collective act, and it is justified by the values of the collectivity and the mutual engagements of its members. In this essay I want first to describe the social processes by which men incur, or come to believe that they have incurred, the obligation to commit such acts. Then I want, very tentatively, to say something about the status of the obligations thus incurred.

The process by which obligations are incurred and the process by which they come to be felt are not the same, or not necessarily the same. They are similar, however, in at least one respect: they are both social processes.[2] They occur in groups, and they can both occur simultaneously in different groups of different shapes and sizes. The duty to disobey arises when such processes are more successful (have greater moral impact) in parties, congregations, sects, movements, unions, or clubs than in states or churches. This happens often in human history, but precisely what is involved when it does needs to be carefully stated.

Obligations can arise in groups of two, between friends, partners, or lovers. But I am chiefly concerned with those which arise in groups of three or more, groups of a more general social, political, or religious nature. These can be obligations to the group as a whole (including oneself), or to the other members, or to the ideal the group stands for or claims to embody. In practice, none of these occurs in pure form; obligations are generally, perhaps necessarily, admixtures of the three. But they are often described exclusively in terms of the last. Thus men announce that they are bound to God or the higher law, and bound "in conscience," which commonly means as morally sensitive individuals rather than as members. In fact, however, the very word "conscience" implies a shared moral knowledge, and it is probably fair to argue not only that the individual's understanding of God or the higher law is always acquired within a group but also that his obligation to either is at the same time an obligation to the group and to its members. "To be 'true to one's principles,'" Robert Paul Wolff has written, "is either a metaphor or else an elliptical way of describing loyalty to other men who share those principles and are relying upon you to observe them."[3] Perhaps this is exaggerated; clearly people feel that their principles embody what is right, and there is nothing odd or metaphorical about saying that one ought to do what is right or what one thinks is right (though it is not clear that this "ought" implies an obligation).[4] All I want to suggest is that commitments to principles are usually also commitments to other men, from whom or with whom the principles have been learned and by whom they are enforced.

This becomes clear, I think, if one examines cases in which ideals are renounced or "sold out." For in all such cases it is individuals or groups of individuals who feel, and can plausibly be said to have been, betrayed. To "sell out" is to renounce heretical ideals for the sake of orthodox ones (but actually, it is generally suggested, for the sake of material gain) or to desert a small nonconformist group and join or rejoin society at large. Most likely, as the common descriptions of this common phenomenon suggest, it is to do both. "An affront to God and an injury to His congregation"—this is the way one's former colleagues describe a conversion to religious orthodoxy. And if God alone can judge the affront, they can rightly weigh the injury, taking into account the kind of commitment which had been made, the expectations which had been aroused, the ridicule to which they are (or are not) subjected, the possible weakening of their community, and so on.[5] Similarly, but more loosely, an artist who "sells out" by "going commercial" is not merely giving up an ideal; he is giving up an ideal to which others still adhere, and those others are his former colleagues. His offense, in their eyes, is not only his betrayal of Art but also his betrayal of them. He injures the cause of Art, they would claim, both in its ideal form and in its concrete social manifestation.

The individual involved, of course, may be doing or think he is doing no such thing. He may have changed his mind for good reasons. And he may believe (rightly, I think) that there is or ought to be some due process whereby he can announce this change of mind, explain its reasons, and so escape the charge of betraying his former colleagues. But however far his obligations extend, insofar as he is obligated at all it is to other men as well as to ideals. Indeed, to think of the effect of his actions upon the ideal he once espoused, which is surely a necessary part of any due process of renunciation or withdrawal, is also to think of its effect upon those who still hold fast to that ideal.

Obligation, then, begins with membership, but membership in the broadest sense, for there are a great variety of formal and informal ways of living within a particular circle of action and commitment. Membership itself can begin with birth. Then the sense of obligation is acquired simply through socialization; it is the product and most often the intended product of religious or political education, of incessant and unrelenting communal pressure, of elaborate rites of passage, periodic ceremonial communions, and so on. One does not acquire any real obligations, however, simply by being born or by submitting to socialization within a particular group. These come only when to the fact of membership there is added the fact of willful membership. Different groups, of course, define willfulness in different ways, some in such minimal ways that willful membership becomes nothing more than continued membership after a certain age, some in such maximal ways that even formal adherence by an adult is inadequate without a public profession of the faith or a period of intensive participation in specified group activities. Sixteenth- and seventeenth-century protests against infant baptism depended upon a maximum definition of individual willfulness, as did Lenin's attack upon the Menshevik view of party membership. And willfulness can be carried even further. Elaborate tests of would-be members, frightening initiation ceremonies, solemn oaths: these mechanisms of the secret society and the revolutionary brotherhood raise to the highest level the individual's sense of having made a choice of enormous personal significance and thereby assumed the most profound obligations.[6]

In general, well-established groups, especially those like the state, which claim to be coterminous with society as a whole, are likely to defend the minimum definition, assume the commitment of their members, and punish those who disobey. Radical or nonconformist groups, precisely because they cannot make the assumption or guarantee the punishment, are likely to require that commitments take the form of explicit and public professions or acts. Through such professions and acts men can and do take on obligations to disobey the rules of the more inclusive group and also accept in advance the risks of their disobedience.

There is also a third sort of group, not sufficiently organized to make any precise determinations as to the character of membership. Disobedient citizens sometimes say that they are obligated by their membership in the "human community" or by their "solidarity with the oppressed." These obligations, if they exist at all, must be said to be universal (and men have indeed been punished for "crimes against humanity"). But they are generally cultivated in relatively small groups, often themselves loosely constituted, whose members can plausibly accuse one another, but not everyone else, of selling out when they fail to live up to their commitments. Since the community which is presumably being sold out is not the smaller but the larger group, which does not have any concrete existence and is only an aspiration, it is difficult to see how or whether anyone else can have made a commitment or what his betrayal would involve.[7] It must be said that efforts to enforce such obligations by individuals against their own states, or by groups of states against individuals, are really efforts to create them. Insofar as these efforts win general support, insofar as an entity like "humanity" acquires some "collective conscience" and some legal and institutional structure, real obligations are in fact incurred by membership. Obviously in such an absolutely inclusive community the willfulness of individuals will play an absolutely minimal part. Humanity can indeed be renounced, but only by becoming a criminal of the very worst sort, by turning oneself into what Locke called a "savage beast." At the present time, since no group exists which can satisfactorily define crimes against humanity, "savage beasts" are necessarily punished ex post facto, not for betraying humanity, but in the hope of creating a humanity whose members are capable of recognizing treason.

The state itself can sometimes be imagined as an ideal or potential community, obligating its members to oppose those authorities who act legally but (it is thought) immorally in its name. Thus those men who disobey the commands of a collaborationist government after military defeat, or of a satellite government after some less formal capitulation, often claim that their state has been betrayed and that they are obligated by their previous membership and driven by their patriotism to resistance. But they cannot claim that all their fellow citizens are similarly obligated. In the aftermath of such struggles, if the resistance is successful, active collaborators may be punished (the legal basis for such punishment is unclear enough), but nothing can be done to those who merely declined to join the fight.[8] They had never incurred any duty to do so. On the other hand, those who did join and subsequently deserted can rightly be said to have broken tangible and morally significant commitments. Thus a leader of the French Resistance, defending the execution of a deserter: "In the Maquis each man had chosen his own lot, fashioned his destiny with his own hands, picked his own name. Everyone had accepted in advance and without question all possible risks."[9] The same obviously cannot be said of Frenchmen in general.

To insist that obligations can only derive from willful undertakings is to restate the theory of the social contract. This has very interesting consequences given the rough typology of groups and kinds of membership just outlined. For contract theory clearly applies best to those sects, congregations, parties, movements, unions, and clubs in which individual choices are made explicit, acted out in some public fashion. It is most useful in discussing what are commonly called secondary associations, less useful (though by no means of no use at all) in discussing larger groups like states and established churches or vague and inclusive entities like humanity. Indeed, if the contract is taken at all seriously, it is difficult to avoid the conclusion that groups in which willfulness is heightened and maximized can rightfully impose greater obligations upon their members than can those catholic religious and political associations where membership is, for all practical purposes, inherited. Of course, inherited membership is often seconded by voluntary participation; in such cases the sense of obligation, as well as the obligation itself, is probably strongest of all. But even participation is likely to be more active and willful and so a more satisfactory token of continuing consent in nonconformist than in established and socially orthodox groups. Day-to-day procedures will be less conventionalized, the modes of participation and communion less habitual. In short, it is possible to conclude from contract theory, as Jean Jacques Rousseau did, that small societies are (generally) morally superior to large ones. For is it not the case that obligations incurred within some Protestant sect, derived from an explicit covenant, and sustained by a continual round of activity, ought to take precedence over obligations incurred in society at large, derived from "tacit" consent, and sustained by mere residence or occasional, largely passive, participation? I do not want to attempt an answer to that question immediately; perhaps there are good reasons for the negative answer conventionally given. But I do want to make two points: first, that obligations are in fact incurred within groups of these different sorts; second, that the conventionally assigned relative weights of these different obligations are not obviously accurate.

The duty to disobey (as well as the possibility of selling out) arises when obligations incurred in some small group come into conflict with obligations incurred in a larger, more inclusive group, generally the state. When the small group is called a secondary association, it is being suggested that there is no point at issue here. Secondary associations ought to yield without argument, conflict, or moral tension to primary ones.[10] This is true only of associations clearly secondary, that is, with purposes or ideals which do not bring them into conflict with the larger society. Rotarians cannot sell out.[11] But there exist in every society groups which may be called "secondary associations with claims to primacy." Serious conflict begins when groups of this sort are formed and their claims announced. But here a crucial distinction must be made: these claims can be of two very different kinds. Some groups announce what are in effect total claims. Their members are obligated, whenever commanded, to challenge the established legal system, to overthrow and replace one government with another, to attack the very existence of the larger society. These are revolutionary groups. There are others, however, that make only partial claims. They demand that the larger society recognize their primacy in some particular area of social or political life and so limit its own. They require of their members disobedience at certain moments, not at every moment, the refusal of particular legal commands, not of every legal command.

It is worth insisting upon the great difference between such groups and between the assertions they make, for defenders of state sovereignty often confuse them, arguing that any challenge to constituted authority is implicitly revolutionary and any group which claims to authorize such challenges necessarily subversive. They thus assign the labels "rebel" and "subversive" to all sorts of people who explicitly reject them. When this is done by officials of the state, the labels often turn out to be accurate, since the men who originally chose not to revolt are eventually forced to do so in self-defense. But there is considerable evidence to suggest that the state can live with, even if it chooses not to accommodate, groups with partial claims against itself. The disobedience of the members of such groups will be intermittent and limited; it is unlikely to be conspiratorial in any sense; it does not usually involve any overt resistance to whatever acts of law enforcement the public authorities feel to be necessary (unless these are radically disproportionate to the "offense"). Such disobedience does not, in fact, challenge the existence of the larger society, only its authority in this or that case or type of case or over persons of this or that sort. It does not seek to replace one sovereign power with another, only to call into question the precise range and incidence of sovereignty. This is not revolution but civil disobedience, which can best be understood, I think, as the acting out of a partial claim against the state.

Limited claims against larger societies can themselves be of two kinds. They can involve assertions that the larger society cannot make demands of a certain sort against *anyone,* or they can involve claims for exemptions for the members (and the future members) of the smaller society. When a man refuses to register for military service, without challenging state authority in any other sphere, he may be saying that the state cannot require anyone to fight on its behalf or to fight this or that particular sort of war, or he may be saying that people like himself cannot be so required. The second statement generally accompanies acts of conscientious objection, which represent only one kind of civil disobedience.

The larger society can always recognize the claims of smaller groups and so relieve their members from the burdens and risks of disobedience. Indeed, the historical basis of liberalism is in large part simply a series of such recognitions. Thus the limited disobedience of religious sectarians was transformed into mere nonconformity when the state decided to tolerate the sects. Tolerance required a limit on the power of the state, a recognition that with regard to religious worship any church or sect could rightfully claim primacy. Contemporary conscientious objectors are also tolerated nonconformists, but here the tolerance is of a different sort. It is a recognition of the claims of a particular type of person (or of particular groups of people) rather than of the claims of any person (or group) in a particular area. There is no necessary logical restriction on either type of toleration: the state could withdraw all its claims from an infinite number of areas, or it could add to every one of its laws a provision specifying that conscientious disobedience cannot be punished.[12] But few states seem likely to move very far in either of these logically possible directions, doubtless for good reasons.

What is the situation of men who join groups with limited claims to primacy in states where such claims are not recognized? It is a situation which political philosophers have never adequately described—though Rousseau surely understood the possibility of divided allegiance and divided men and bent all his efforts to avoid both. Locke provides a convenient outline of the possibilities more generally thought to be available: (1) A man can be a *citizen;* this involves a full recognition of the primacy of his society and its government. Certain areas are set beyond the reach of the government, but in such a way as to bar any possible obligations against it. There are only rights and ultimately, so far as action goes, only one right, the right of rebellion. Hence, (2) a man can be a *rebel,* seeking to overthrow and replace a particular government and its laws. These are the only two possibilities available to members of the larger society. But Locke suggests two further options for those persons who do not wish to be members: (3) A man can be an *emigrant,* willfully withdrawing from the larger society and physically leaving its territory. Emigration is the only due process through which social obligations can be renounced, for the rebel is still bound, if not to his government, then to society itself. Finally, (4) a man can be an *alien* who, having left the society of his fathers, fails to commit himself to any other and lives here or there at the discretion of the public authorities. An alien, for Locke, has obligations, for he is afforded protection within some particular society and tacitly consents in return to obey its laws. He presumably has rights, at least in theory, since rights are natural. He must even possess, I think, the right to rebel, though it is not clear that he possesses this right as fully as citizens do: he cannot protest if his consent is not asked to government or taxation. This appears to be the single most important difference between aliens and citizens.

Now the member of a group with partial claims to primacy falls into none of these categories. His loyalties are divided, so he is not in any simple sense a citizen. He refuses to call himself a rebel, and with good reason, for he seeks no total change in the government, no transformation of state or society (though he would surely claim the right to rebel, in Locke's sense, given the conditions under which Locke permits rebellion). He is not an emigrant, since he does not leave, though joining such a group may well constitute a kind of internal emigration. He is not an alien, for while an alien can always leave, he cannot demand to stay on conditions of his own choosing.

Yet the situation of such a man—obligated to obey because of his membership in a larger society, obligated to disobey (sometimes) because of his membership in a smaller one—is, for all its tensions, very common in history and has often been fairly stable over long

periods of time. It is the situation of any person who, like Sophocles'
Antigone, retains strong tribal or clan loyalties while becoming a
member of some (almost any) political order.[13] It is virtually institu-
tionalized in feudal systems.[14] It was lived through with extraordi-
nary intensity by early modern Protestants and has been lived
through since with greater or lesser intensity by a considerable variety of religious groups (including Roman Catholics, for Rousseau the
visible embodiments of double obligation and moral division)—even
in liberal societies, which have recognized some but not all the
claims of pious brethren of this or that persuasion. It was the situation of European socialists during the period when their parties and
movements had ceased to be revolutionary but had not yet accepted
the status of secondary associations. (Otto Kirchheimer describes
German Social-Democracy as a "loyalty-absorbing counterorganiza-
tion."[15]) It is often the situation of trade unionists, especially when
their country is at war. It is the situation today of all those persons
who object to military service on other than the permitted religious
grounds. It is, despite considerable confusion, increasingly the situation of many members of the American civil-rights movement.

What all these oddly assorted people have in common is this: none
of them admits without qualification the political sovereignty or
moral supremacy of the larger society of which they are members.
None of them absolutely denies that sovereignty or supremacy. They
are, then, partial members; they are simultaneously partial emi-
grants, partial aliens, partial rebels. The very existence of such people—even more, their obvious moral seriousness—ought to call into
question the conventional description of citizenship as involving an
absolute commitment (it is sometimes said, "under God") to obey the
laws. Surely such a commitment will never be found among every one
of those persons who consider themselves, with reason, citizens of the
state. For the processes through which men incur obligations are un-
avoidably pluralistic. Even or perhaps especially in a liberal society,
which allows considerable room for divergent groups and recognizes
many of their claims, what might be called the incidence of obligation
is bound to be uneven, the obligations themselves at least sometimes
contradictory. Unless the state deliberately inhibits the normal processes of group formation, and does so with greater success than has
ever yet been achieved, it will always be confronted by citizens who
believe themselves to be, and may actually be, obligated to disobey.
As J. N. Figgis wrote: "The theory of sovereignty . . . is in reality no
more than a venerable superstition. . . . As a fact it is as a series of

groups that our social life presents itself, all having some of the qualities of public law and most of them showing clear signs of a life of their own."[16]

Many political philosophers have insisted that there exists a prima facie obligation to obey the laws of the most inclusive organized society of which one is a member, that is, for most men, the state.[17] This is not unreasonable, so long as the state provides equally to all its members certain essential services. It is not unreasonable even though the state maintains a monopoly of such services and tolerates no competition, for it may be that the monopoly is itself essential to the provision of the services. But the existence of a prima facie obligation to obey means no more than that disobedience must always be justified. First explanations are owed to those of one's fellow citizens who do not join in, who remain obedient. I think it can be argued that membership (that is, morally serious membership) in groups with partial claims to primacy is always a possible explanation.

But I want to attempt a somewhat stronger argument than this, loosely derived from the preceding discussion of the uneven incidence of obligation in any larger society. I want to suggest that men have a prima facie obligation to honor the engagements they have explicitly made, to defend the groups and uphold the ideals to which they have committed themselves, even against the state, so long as their disobedience of laws or legally authorized commands does not threaten the very existence of the larger society or endanger the lives of its citizens. Sometimes it is obedience to the state, when one has a duty to disobey, that must be justified. First explanations are owed to one's brethren, colleagues, or comrades. Their usual form is an argument that physical security or public health or some other such necessity of the common life—which the smaller groups cannot supply, which is actually supplied by the state—is being threatened or is likely to be threatened by particular acts of disobedience, however limited their scope. This, of course, is precisely what is asserted (usually by an official of the state) in every case of disobedience, but it is not necessarily asserted rightly. Indeed, there is very little evidence which suggests that carefully limited, morally serious civil disobedience undermines the legal system or endangers physical security.[18] One can imagine situations in which the acting out of partial claims might encourage or inspire the acting out of total claims. But the two sorts of action remain distinct. It may be necessary for a man contemplating civil disobedience to worry about the possibilities of revolutionary violence, but only if such possibilities actually exist. It is by no means necessary for him to reflect upon the purely theoretical possibility that his action might be universalized, that all men might break the laws or claim exemptions from them. For his action implies nothing more than that those men ought to do so who have acquired obligations to do so. And the acquiring of such obligations is a serious, long-term business which is not in fact undertaken by everybody.

The state can thus be described as a purely external limit on group action, but it must be added that the precise point at which the limit becomes effective cannot be left for state officials to decide. For them, the law must be the limit. At the same time, it must be the claim of the disobedient members that the law is overextended, that its sphere ought to be restricted in some fashion, that this activity or this type of person should be exempted, at this particular moment or for all time. There can be no possible judge of this disagreement. All that can be said is that the moral seriousness of the disobedient members is evidenced in part by their respect for those genuine goods the state provides not only to themselves but to everyone. To argue that the state does not provide such goods at all, or that it denies them entirely to particular sections of the population, is to justify, or to try to justify, unlimited and uncivil disobedience, that is, revolution. Revolution always requires (and generally gets) some such special justification.

There are two other ways of describing the state which appear to argue against the claim that disobedience can ever be a prima facie obligation. The first is to insist that the state is itself a group, that its members too are willful members who have incurred obligations of the most serious kind. It was the original purpose of social-contract theory to uphold just this conception of the state. But there are serious problems here. Since for many men there are no practical alternatives to state membership, the willfulness of that membership seems to have only minimal moral significance. A theory like Locke's requires the argument that one can always leave the state; residence itself, therefore, can meaningfully be described as a choice. That argument has some value—it may even be true that more people move across state frontiers now (though not always voluntarily) than in Locke's time—yet one cannot always leave, and so we would be wrong, I think, to base the weightiest political obligations on the non-act of not-leaving. There is a better way of describing the willfulness of state membership: that is to take very seriously the possibility of joining secondary associations with limited claims to primacy. Such engagements represent, as I have already suggested, a kind of internal emigration, and so long as the processes of group formation are open, and whether or not the frontiers are open, they offer real (though partial) alternatives to state membership as it is conventionally described. It is not the case, of course, that whoever fails to seize upon these alternatives thereby declares himself a member of the state and accepts all the attendant responsibilities. But membership is established as a moral option by the existence of alternatives. Thus, the possibility of becoming a conscientious objector establishes the *possibility* of incurring an obligation to fight in the army. But if the groups within which men learn to object are repressed by the state, that possibility disappears, for in one important sense at least the state is no longer a voluntary association.[19] Only if the possible legitimacy of countergroups with limited claims is recognized and admitted can the state be regarded as a group of consenting citizens.

But the obligations of citizens to the state can be derived in yet another way: not from their willfulness but from its value. "If all communities aim at some good," wrote Aristotle, "the state or political community, which is the highest of all, and which embraces all the rest, aims, and in a greater degree than any other, at the highest good."[20] Obviously, groups which aim at the highest good take priority over groups which seek lower or partial goods. There are two major difficulties, however, with Aristotle's description. First of all, it is not the case that the state necessarily embraces all other communities. A state with an established church and no legal provision for religious toleration obviously excludes a dissenting sect. Groups with universalist or international pretensions, like the Catholic church or any early twentieth-century socialist party, necessarily exclude themselves. Political or religious communities which oppose war are in no simple sense "embraced" by states which fight wars. It is precisely the nature of secondary associations with claims to primacy that they cannot and do not exist wholly within the established political or legal frame. Second, while the state may well provide or seek to provide goods for all its members, it is not clear that these add up to or include the highest good. Perhaps they are goods of the lowest common denominator and only for this reason available to all, for it may be that the highest good can be pursued only in small groups— in pietist sects or utopian settlements, for example, or, as Aristotle himself suggested, in philosophic dialogue. In any case, men do not agree as to the nature of the highest good, and this fact is enormously significant for the processes of group formation. Groups are formed for a great variety of reasons, but one of the chief reasons is to advocate or act out ("without tarrying for the magistrate," as a late sixteenth-century Puritan minister wrote) a new conception of the highest good, a conception at which the state does not aim, and perhaps cannot. To form such a group or to join one is to reject Aristotle's argument and renounce whatever obligation is implied by it. I fail to see any reason why this is not an option available to any morally serious man.

In the argument thus far, I have attached a great deal of weight to the phrase "morally serious." Obviously, the term is not easy to define, nor the quality easy to measure. Yet frivolous or criminal disobedience cannot be justified by membership in a group. There are obligations among thieves, but not prima facie obligations against the state. This is true, first of all, because the activities of thieves endanger the security of us all. But it is also true because a robbers' gang does not make claims to primacy. Thieves do not seek to limit the authority of the sovereign state; they seek to evade it. But there is nothing evasive about civil disobedience: a public claim against the state is publicly acted out. This willingness to act in public and to offer explanations to other people suggests also a willingness to reflect upon and worry about the possible consequences of the action for the public as a whole. Neither of these by themselves legitimate the action; but they do signal the moral seriousness of the group commitment that legitimates it.[21]

Frivolous disobedience can also never be a duty, and so groups that do not encourage an awareness in their members of the purposes and actions to which they may become committed cannot commit them. Awareness of this sort would appear to be required by social-contract theory; even the notion of tacit consent implies that there exists some knowledge of the duties being incurred. Nor, it seems to me, are the requirements of the theory entirely satisfied if such knowledge is but glimpsed at one brief moment in time. Continued awareness, a kind of shared self-consciousness, is necessary before the consent and participation of individuals carry sufficient moral weight to establish obligations—or, at any rate, to establish such obligations as I am trying to defend. A morally serious member of a group with partial claims may, then, be described as follows: he joins the group voluntarily, knowing what membership involves; he devotes time and energy to its inner life, sharing in the making of decisions; he acts publicly in its name or in the name of its ideals. Such a person—not any person—is obligated to act as he does, unless he is given good reasons why he ought not to do so.

The problem of civil disobedience needs to be placed squarely in the context of group formation, growth, tension, and conflict. There is a sociology of disobedience, which has greater relevance for philosophy than has generally been thought; it helps establish the proper units of analysis. Now these units doubtless have their limits, for it is true that there come moments when individuals must make choices or sustain actions alone—or rather, and this is not at all the same thing, when they must endure the anguish of loneliness. The state always seeks to isolate its disobedient citizens, because it is far more likely to bend their wills to its own if it can break the cohesion of the group which initially planned the disobedience and convince its members that they are members no longer. But this only suggests that the men who run prisons are always very much aware of the sociology of disobedience. Surely philosophers should be no less so.

The heroic encounter between sovereign individual and sovereign state, if it ever took place, would be terrifyingly unequal. If disobedience depended upon a conscience really private, it might always be justified and yet never occur. Locke understood this very well, for even while he proclaimed the right of individuals to rebel, he recognized that "the right to do so will not easily engage them in a contest, wherein they are sure to perish."[22] Rebellion, he thought, is only possible when it engages "the whole body" of the people. But clearly, rebellion and, even more, civil disobedience are most often the work of groups of much more limited extent. Clearly, too, it is not the mere individual right to rebel, unchanged in groups large or small, that sustains the enterprise but, rather, the mutual undertakings of the participants. Without this mutuality, very few men would ever join the "contest"—not because of the fear of being killed but because of the greater fear of being alone. "This is what is most difficult," wrote Jean Le Meur, the young French army officer who was imprisoned for refusing to fight in Algeria, "being cut off from the fraternity, being locked up in a monologue, being incomprehensible." And then: "Do tell the others that this is not a time to let me down."[23]

All this is not to suggest that there is anything unreal about individual responsibility. But this is always responsibility *to someone else* and it is always learned *with someone else.*[24] An individual whose moral experiences never reached beyond "monologue" would know nothing at all about responsibility and would have none. Such a man might well have rights, including the right to rebel, but his possession of the right to rebel would be purely theoretical; he would never become a rebel. No political theory which does not move beyond rights to duties, beyond monologue to fraternal discussion, debate, and resolution, can ever explain what men actually do when they disobey or rebel, or why they do so. Nor can it help us very much to weigh the rightness or wrongness of what they do.

NOTES

1. Hugo Bedau, "On Civil Disobedience," *Journal of Philosophy* 57 (1961) 663.

2. The best description of these processes is probably still Emile Durkheim's *Moral Education* (trans. E. K. Wilson and H. Schnurer; New York: Free Press, 1961).

3. Robert Paul Wolff, "An Analysis of the Concept of Political Loyalty," in *Political Man and Social Man* (ed. Robert Paul Wolff; New York: Random House, 1966) 224.

4. See Alexander Sesonske, *Value and Obligation* (New York: Oxford University Press, 1964) 20–23 and passim.

5. Where such judgments cannot be made at all, there is no obligation. And this means that obligations are always shared among men, who must judge one another. "The only obligation which I have a right to assume," wrote Thoreau, "is to do at any time what I think right." But when, in jail, he greeted the visiting Emerson with the famous question, "What are you doing out there?" he clearly implied the existence of a common obligation. Common to whom? Common at least to New England philosophers, one of whom was failing to meet it. Emerson believed the same thing when he spoke in his lecture on the Fugitive Slave Law of the "disastrous defection of the men of letters" from the cause of freedom (*The Complete Essays and Other Writings of Ralph Waldo Emerson* [New York: Modern Library, 1940] 867).

6. Eric Hobsbawm, *Primitive Rebels* (New York: Frederick A. Praeger, 1963) chapter 9; for some examples of secret oaths, see his appendix 13.

7. Sesonske, *Value and Obligation,* 107.

8. Henry L. Mason, *The Purge of Dutch Quislings* (The Hague: Nijhoff, 1952) chapter 2.

9. Guillain de Benouville, *The Unknown Warriors* (New York: Simon & Schuster, 1949) 220.

10. S. I. Benn and R. S. Peters, *The Principles of Political Thought* (New York: Free Press, 1965) chapter 12.

11. People who accuse trade-union leaders of selling out are, in effect, accusing them of acting like leaders of secondary associations, the implication of their accusation being that the union (or the labor movement generally) is something more than secondary.

12. Bedau, "Civil Disobedience," 655.

13. The conflict in Sophocles' play is, of course, between primary groups. In general, conflicts between groups of relatives or friends and the state take forms similar to those described above, especially in modern times when

such alliances tend increasingly to be voluntary. E. M. Forster's statement that "if I had to choose between betraying my country and betraying my friend, I hope I should have the guts to betray my country" (*Two Cheers for Democracy* [New York: Harcourt, Brace & Co., 1951] 78) is roughly analogous to the sorts of assertions sometimes made on behalf of groups. But it is an extreme statement and has reference to exceptional cases. Most often, the choice is between betraying one's friends (or colleagues) and *disobeying the laws* of one's country. Antigone's act is not treason, in any usual interpretation of that tricky term.

14. See Marc Bloch, *Feudal Society* (trans. L. A. Manyon; Chicago: University of Chicago Press, 1961) chapters 9–17.

15. Otto Kirchheimer, *Political Justice* (Princeton: Princeton University Press, 1961) 9. Trotsky takes an even stronger position, with regard not to Social Democracy but to the working class, and then draws an important conclusion: "In all decisive questions, people feel their class membership considerably more profoundly and more directly than their membership in 'society.' . . . The moral norm becomes the more categorical the less it is 'obligatory' upon all" (*The Basic Writings of Trotsky* [ed. Irving Howe; New York: Random House, 1963] 378).

16. J. N. Figgis, *Churches in the Modern State* (London: Longmans, Green & Co., 1914) 224. See also G. D. H. Cole, "Conflicting Social Obligations," *Proceedings of the Aristotelian Society* 15 (1915), and idem, "Loyalties," *Proceedings of the Aristotelian Society* 26 (1926).

17. See, for example, W. D. Ross, *The Right and the Good* (Oxford: Clarendon Press, 1930) 27–28; and discussion in Richard Wasserstrom, "Disobeying the Law," *Journal of Philosophy* 57 (1961) 647.

18. It is often enough said that disobedience even of bad laws undermines the habit of law abidance and so endangers that fundamental order upon which civilized life depends. But I have never seen this argued with careful attention to some particular body of evidence. In the absence of such an argument, I would be inclined to agree with David Spitz that there are clearly *some* laws obedience to which is not required for the maintenance of social order. Even more important, perhaps, there are many laws which can be disobeyed by *some men,* without prejudice to social order (Spitz, "Democracy and the Problem of Civil Disobedience," in *Essays in the Liberal Idea of Freedom* [Tucson: University of Arizona Press, 1964] 74–75).

19. I argue for the pluralist basis of conscientious objection in the sixth of the essays in *Obligations* (Cambridge, Mass.: Harvard University Press, 1982), and of citizenship in the tenth.

20. Quoted in Benn and Peters, *Principles,* 315, and discussed, 315–25.

21. Secret societies, if they are not criminal, are implicitly revolutionary; the moral seriousness of their members must be signaled differently.

22. John Locke, *The Second Treatise of Government,* paragraph 208.

23. Jean Le Meur, "The Story of a Responsible Act," in *Political Man* (ed. Wolff) 204, 205.

24. Individual integrity, honor, or "authenticity" is different from this, though it is sometimes described, metaphorically, as responsibility to oneself. In the ninth essay in *Obligations,* I discuss possible conflicts between obligation and personal honor.

8

*Letter from Birmingham City Jail**

Martin Luther King, Jr.

This selection begins with a letter from eight Alabama clergymen to Reverend Martin Luther King, and gives his famous reply in his "Letter from Birmingham City Jail," explaining why he had engaged in civil disobedience.

April 12, 1963

We the undersigned clergymen are among those who, in January, issued "An Appeal for Law and Order and Common Sense," in dealing with racial problems in Alabama. We expressed understanding that honest convictions in racial matters could properly be pursued in the courts, but urged that decisions of those courts should in the meantime be peacefully obeyed.

Since that time there had been some evidence of increased forbearance and a willingness to face facts. Responsible citizens have undertaken to work on various problems which cause racial friction and unrest. In Birmingham, recent public events have given indication that we all have opportunity for a new constructive and realistic approach to racial problems.

However, we are now confronted by a series of demonstrations by some of our Negro citizens, directed and led in part by outsiders. We recognize the natural impatience of people who feel that their hopes are slow in being realized. But we are convinced that these demonstrations are unwise and untimely.

---

*Published in *Why We Can't Wait* by Martin Luther King, Jr. (1963) 152–68.

We agree rather with certain local Negro leadership which has called for honest and open negotiation of racial issues in our area. And we believe this kind of facing of issues can best be accomplished by citizens of our own metropolitan area, white and Negro, meeting with their knowledge and experience of the local situation. All of us need to face that responsibility and find proper channels for its accomplishment.

Just as we formerly pointed out that "hatred and violence have no sanction in our religious and political traditions," we also point out that such actions as incite to hatred and violence, however technically peaceful those actions may be, have not contributed to the resolution of our local problems. We do not believe that these days of new hope are days when extreme measures are justified in Birmingham.

We commend the community as a whole, and the local news media and law enforcement officials in particular, on the calm manner in which these demonstrations have been handled. We urge the public to continue to show restraint should the demonstrations continue, and the law enforcement officials to remain calm and continue to protect our city from violence.

We further strongly urge our own Negro community to withdraw support from these demonstrations, and to unite locally in working peacefully for a better Birmingham. When rights are consistently denied, a cause should be pressed in the courts and in negotiations among local leaders, and not in the streets. We appeal to both our white and Negro citizenry to observe the principles of law and order and common sense.

Signed by:

C. C. J. CARPENTER, D.D., LL.D., Bishop of Alabama

JOSEPH A. DURICK, D.D., Auxiliary Bishop, Diocese of Mobile-Birmingham

RABBI MILTON L. GRAFMAN, Temple Emanu-El, Birmingham, Alabama

BISHOP PAUL HARDIN, Bishop of the Alabama–West Florida Conference of the Methodist Church

BISHOP NOLAN B. HARMON, Bishop of the North Alabama Conference of the Methodist Church

GEORGE M. MURRAY, D.D., LL.D., Bishop Coadjutor, Episcopal Diocese of Alabama

EDWARD V. RAMAGE, Moderator, Synod of the Alabama Presbyterian Church in the United States

EARL STALLINGS, Pastor, First Baptist Church, Birmingham, Alabama

MARTIN LUTHER KING, JR.
Birmingham City Jail
April 16, 1963

My dear Fellow Clergymen,

While confined here in the Birmingham City Jail, I came across your recent statement calling our present activities "unwise and untimely." Seldom, if ever, do I pause to answer criticism of my work and ideas. If I sought to answer all of the criticisms that cross my desk, my secretaries would be engaged in little else in the course of the day and I would have no time for constructive work. But since I feel that you are men of genuine goodwill and your criticisms are sincerely set forth, I would like to answer your statement in what I hope will be patient and reasonable terms.

I think I should give the reason for my being in Birmingham, since you have been influenced by the argument of "outsiders coming in." I have the honor of serving as president of the Southern Christian Leadership Conference, an organization operating in every Southern state with headquarters in Atlanta, Georgia. We have some eighty-five affiliate organizations all across the South—one being the Alabama Christian Movement for Human Rights. Whenever necessary and possible we share staff, educational, and financial resources with our affiliates. Several months ago our local affiliate here in Birmingham invited us to be on call to engage in a nonviolent direct action program if such were deemed necessary. We readily consented and when the hour came we lived up to our promises. So I am here, along with several members of my staff, because we were invited here. I am here because I have basic organizational ties here. Beyond this, I am in Birmingham because injustice is here. Just as the eighth century prophets left their little villages and carried their "thus saith the Lord" far beyond the boundaries of their home town, and just as the Apostle Paul left his little village of Tarsus and carried the gospel of Jesus Christ to practically every hamlet and city of the Graeco-Roman world, I too am compelled to carry the gospel of freedom beyond my particular home town. Like Paul, I must constantly respond to the Macedonian call for aid.

Moreover, I am cognizant of the interrelatedness of all communities and states. I cannot sit idly by in Atlanta and not be concerned about what happens in Birmingham. Injustice anywhere is a threat to justice everywhere. We are caught in an inescapable network of mutuality tied in a single garment of destiny. Whatever affects one directly affects all indirectly. Never again can we afford to live with the narrow, provincial "outside agitator" idea. Anyone who lives inside the United States can never be considered an outsider anywhere in the country.

You deplore the demonstrations that are presently taking place in Birmingham. But I am sorry that your statement did not express a similar concern for the conditions that brought the demonstrations into being. I am sure that each of you would want to go beyond the superficial social analyst who looks merely at effects, and does not grapple with underlying causes. I would not hesitate to say that it is unfortunate that so-called demonstrations are taking place in Birmingham at this time, but I would say in more emphatic terms that it is even more unfortunate that the white power structure of this city left the Negro community with no other alternative.

In any nonviolent campaign there are four basic steps: (1) collection of the facts to determine whether injustices are alive; (2) negotiation; (3) self-purification; and (4) direct action. We have gone through all of these steps in Birmingham. There can be no gainsaying of the fact that racial injustice engulfs this community. Birmingham is probably the most thoroughly segregated city in the United States. Its ugly record of police brutality is known in every section of this country. Its unjust treatment of Negroes in the courts is a notorious reality. There have been more unsolved bombings of Negro homes and churches in Birmingham than any city in this nation. These are the hard, brutal, and unbelievable facts. On the basis of these conditions Negro leaders sought to negotiate with the city fathers. But the political leaders consistently refused to engage in good faith negotiation.

Then came the opportunity last September to talk with some of the leaders of the economic community. In these negotiating sessions certain promises were made by the merchants—such as the promise to remove the humiliating racial signs from the stores. On the basis of these promises Rev. Shuttlesworth and the leaders of the Alabama Christian Movement for Human Rights agreed to call a moratorium on any type of demonstrations. As the weeks and months unfolded we realized that we were the victims of a broken promise. The signs remained. As in so many experiences of the past we were confronted with blasted hopes, and the dark shadow of a deep disappointment settled upon us. So we had no alternative except that of preparing for direct action, whereby we would present our very bodies as a means of laying our case before the conscience of the local and national community. We were not unmindful of the difficulties involved. So we decided to go through a process of self-purification. We started having workshops on nonviolence and repeatedly asked ourselves the questions, "Are you able to accept blows without retaliating?" "Are you able to endure the ordeals of jail?"

We decided to set our direct action program around the Easter season, realizing that with the exception of Christmas, this was the largest shopping period of the year. Knowing that a strong economic withdrawal program would be the by-product of direct action, we felt that this was the best time to bring pressure on the merchants for the needed changes. Then it occurred to us that the March election was ahead, and so we speedily decided to postpone action until after election day. When we discovered that Mr. Connor was in the run-off, we decided again to postpone action so that the demonstrations could not be used to cloud the issues. At this time we agreed to begin our nonviolent witness the day after the run-off.

This reveals that we did not move irresponsibly into direct action. We too wanted to see Mr. Connor defeated; so we went through postponement after postponement to aid in this community need. After this we felt that direct action could be delayed no longer.

You may well ask, "Why direct action? Why sit-ins, marches, etc.? Isn't negotiation a better path?" You are exactly right in your call for negotiation. Indeed, this is the purpose of direct action. Nonviolent direct action seeks to create such a crisis and establish such creative tension that a community that has constantly refused to negotiate is forced to confront the issue. It seeks so to dramatize the issue that it can no longer be ignored. I just referred to the creation of tension as a part of the work of the nonviolent resister. This may sound rather shocking. But I must confess that I am not afraid of the word tension. I have earnestly worked and preached against violent tension, but there is a type of constructive nonviolent tension that is necessary for growth. Just as Socrates felt that it was necessary to create a tension in the mind so that individuals could rise from the bondage of myths and half-truths to the unfettered realm of creative analysis and objective appraisal, we must see the need of having nonviolent gadflies to create the kind of tension in society that will help men rise from the

dark depths of prejudice and racism to the majestic heights of understanding and brotherhood. So the purpose of the direct action is to
create a situation so crisis-packed that it will inevitably open the
door to negotiation. We, therefore, concur with you in your call for
negotiation. Too long has our beloved Southland been bogged down
in the tragic attempt to live in monologue rather than dialogue.

One of the basic points in your statement is that our acts are untimely. Some have asked, "Why didn't you give the new administration time to act?" The only answer that I can give to this inquiry is
that the new administration must be prodded about us, much as the
outgoing one before it acts. We will be sadly mistaken if we feel that
the election of Mr. Boutwell will bring the millennium to Birmingham. While Mr. Boutwell is much more articulate and gentle than
Mr. Connor, they are both segregationists dedicated to the task of
maintaining the status quo. The hope I see in Mr. Boutwell is that he
will be reasonable enough to see the futility of massive resistance to
desegregation. But he will not see this without pressure from the
devotees of civil rights. My friends, I must say to you that we have not
made a single gain in civil rights without determined legal and nonviolent pressure. History is the long and tragic story of the fact that
privileged groups seldom give up their privileges voluntarily. Individuals may see the moral light and voluntarily give up their unjust
posture; but as Reinhold Niebuhr has reminded us, groups are more
immoral than individuals.

We know through painful experience that freedom is never voluntarily given by the oppressor; it must be demanded by the oppressed. Frankly I have never yet engaged in a direct action
movement that was "well timed," according to the timetable of
those who have not suffered unduly from the disease of segregation. For years now I have heard the word "Wait!" It rings in the ear
of every Negro with a piercing familiarity. This "wait" has almost
always meant "never." It has been a tranquilizing thalidomide,
relieving the emotional stress for a moment, only to give birth to an
ill-formed infant of frustration. We must come to see with the
distinguished jurist of yesterday that "justice too long delayed is
justice denied." We have waited for more than three hundred and
forty years for· our constitutional and God-given rights. The nations of Asia and Africa are moving with jet-like speed toward the
goal of political independence, and we still creep at horse and
buggy pace toward the gaining of a cup of coffee at a lunch counter.

I guess it is easy for those who have never felt the stinging darts of segregation to say wait. But when you have seen vicious mobs lynch your mothers and fathers at will and drown your sisters and brothers at whim; when you have seen hate-filled policemen curse, kick, brutalize, and even kill your black brothers and sisters with impunity; when you see the vast majority of your twenty million Negro brothers smothering in an air-tight cage of poverty in the midst of an affluent society; when you suddenly find your tongue twisted and your speech stammering as you seek to explain to your six-year-old daughter why she can't go to the public amusement park that has just been advertised on television, and see tears welling up in her little eyes when she is told that Funtown is closed to colored children, and see the depressing clouds of inferiority begin to form in her little mental sky, and see her begin to distort her little personality by unconsciously developing a bitterness toward white people; when you have to concoct an answer for a five-year-old son asking in agonizing pathos: "Daddy, why do white people treat colored people so mean?"; when you take a cross country drive and find it necessary to sleep night after night in the uncomfortable corners of your automobile because no motel will accept you; when you are humiliated day in and day out by nagging signs reading "white" men and "colored"; when your first name becomes "nigger" and your middle name becomes "boy" (however old you are) and your last name becomes "John," and when your wife and mother are never given the respected title "Mrs."; when you are harried by day and haunted by night by the fact that you are a Negro, living constantly at tip-toe stance never quite knowing what to expect next, and plagued with inner fears and outer resentments; when you are forever fighting a degenerating sense of "nobodiness"; —then you will understand why we find it difficult to wait. There comes a time when the cup of endurance runs over, and men are no longer willing to be plunged into an abyss of injustice where they experience the bleakness of corroding despair. I hope, sirs, you can understand our legitimate and unavoidable impatience.

You express a great deal of anxiety over our willingness to break laws. This is certainly a legitimate concern. Since we so diligently urge people to obey the Supreme Court's decision of 1954 outlawing segregation in the public schools, it is rather strange and paradoxical to find us consciously breaking laws. One may well ask, "How can you advocate breaking some laws and obeying others?" The answer is found in the fact that there are two types of laws: There are *just* laws and there are *unjust* laws. I would be the first to advocate obeying just laws. One has not only a legal but moral responsibility to obey just laws.

Conversely, one has a moral responsibility to disobey unjust laws. I would agree with Saint Augustine that "An unjust law is no law at all."

Now what is the difference between the two? How does one determine when a law is just or unjust? A just law is a man-made code that squares with the moral law or the law of God. An unjust law is a code that is out of harmony with the moral law. To put it in the terms of Saint Thomas Aquinas, an unjust law is a human law that is not rooted in eternal and natural law. Any law that uplifts human personality is just. Any law that degrades human personality is unjust. All segregation statutes are unjust because segregation distorts the soul and damages the personality. It gives the segregator a false sense of superiority and the segregated a false sense of inferiority. To use the words of Martin Buber, the great Jewish philosopher, segregation substitutes an "I-it" relationship for the "I-thou" relationship, and ends up relegating persons to the status of things. So segregation is not only politically, economically, and sociologically unsound, but it is morally wrong and sinful. Paul Tillich has said that sin is separation. Isn't segregation an existential expression of man's tragic separation, an expression of his awful estrangement, his terrible sinfulness? So I can urge men to obey the 1954 decision of the Supreme Court because it is morally right, and I can urge them to disobey segregation ordinances because they are morally wrong.

Let us turn to a more concrete example of just and unjust laws. An unjust law is a code that a majority inflicts on a minority that is not binding on itself. This is *difference* made legal. On the other hand a just law is a code that a majority compels a minority to follow that it is willing to follow itself. This is *sameness* made legal.

Let me give another explanation. An unjust law is a code inflicted upon a minority which that minority had no part in enacting or creating because they did not have the unhampered right to vote. Who can say the legislature of Alabama which set up the segregation laws was democratically elected? Throughout the state of Alabama all types of conniving methods are used to prevent Negroes from becoming registered voters and there are some counties without a single Negro registered to vote despite the fact that the Negro constitutes a majority of the population. Can any law set up in such a state be considered democratically structured?

These are just a few examples of unjust and just laws. There are some instances when a law is just on its face but unjust in its application. For instance, I was arrested Friday on a charge of parading without a permit. Now there is nothing wrong with an ordinance which requires a permit for a parade, but when the ordinance is used to preserve segregation and to deny citizens the First Amendment privilege of peaceful assembly and peaceful protest, then it becomes unjust.

I hope you can see the distinction I am trying to point out. In no sense do I advocate evading or defying the law as the rabid segregationist would do. This would lead to anarchy. One who breaks an unjust law must do it *openly, lovingly* (not hatefully as the white mothers did in New Orleans when they were seen on television screaming "nigger, nigger, nigger") and with a willingness to accept the penalty. I submit that an individual who breaks a law that conscience tells him is unjust, and willingly accepts the penalty by staying in jail to arouse the conscience of the community over its injustice, is in reality expressing the very highest respect for law.

Of course there is nothing new about this kind of civil disobedience. It was seen sublimely in the refusal of Shadrach, Meshach, and Abednego to obey the laws of Nebuchadnezzar because a higher moral law was involved. It was practiced superbly by the early Christians who were willing to face hungry lions and the excruciating pain of chopping blocks, before submitting to certain unjust laws of the Roman Empire. To a degree academic freedom is a reality today because Socrates practiced civil disobedience.

We can never forget that everything Hitler did in Germany was "legal" and everything the Hungarian freedom fighters did in Hungary was "illegal." It was "illegal" to aid and comfort a Jew in Hitler's Germany. But I am sure that, if I had lived in Germany during that time, I would have aided and comforted my Jewish brothers even though it was illegal. If I lived in a Communist country today where certain principles dear to the Christian faith are suppressed, I believe I would openly advocate disobeying these anti-religious laws.

I must make two honest confessions to you, my Christian and Jewish brothers. First I must confess that over the last few years I have been gravely disappointed with the white moderate. I have almost reached the regrettable conclusion the the Negroes' great stumbling block in the stride toward freedom is not the White Citizens' "Counciler" or the Klu Klux Klanner, but the white moderate who is more devoted to "order" than to justice; who prefers a negative peace which is the absence of tension to a positive peace which is the presence of justice; who constantly says, "I agree with you in the goal you seek, but I can't agree with your methods of direct action"; who paternalistically feels that he can set the timetable for another man's freedom; who lives by the myth of time and who constantly advises the Negro to wait until a "more convenient season." Shallow understanding from people of good will is more frustrating than absolute misunderstanding from people of ill will. Lukewarm acceptance is much more bewildering than outright rejection.

I had hoped that the white moderate would understand that law and order exist for the purpose of establishing justice, and that when they fail to do this they become the dangerously structured dams that block the flow of social progress. I had hoped that the white moderate would understand that the present tension in the South is merely a necessary phase of the transition from an obnoxious negative peace, where the Negro passively accepted his unjust plight, to a substance-filled positive peace, where all men will respect the dignity and worth of human personality. Actually, we who engage in nonviolent direct action are not the creators of tension. We merely bring to the surface the hidden tension that is already alive. We bring it out in the open where it can be seen and dealt with. Like a boil that can never be cured as long as it is covered up but must be opened with all its pus-flowing ugliness to the natural medicines of air and light, injustice must likewise be exposed, with all of the tension its exposing creates, to the light of human conscience and the air of national opinion before it can be cured.

In your statement you asserted that our actions, even though peaceful, must be condemned because they precipitate violence. But can this assertion be logically made? Isn't this like condemning the robbed man because his possession of money precipitated the evil act of robbery? Isn't this like condemning Socrates because his unswerving commitment to truth and his philosophical delvings precipitated the misguided popular mind to make him drink the hemlock? Isn't this like condemning Jesus because His unique God consciousness and never-ceasing devotion to His will precipitated the evil act of crucifixion? We must come to see, as federal courts have consistently affirmed, that it is immoral to urge an individual to withdraw his efforts to gain his basic constitutional rights because the quest precipitates violence. Society must protect the robbed and punish the robber.

I had also hoped that the white moderate would reject the myth of time. I received a letter this morning from a white brother in Texas which said: "All Christians know that the colored people will receive equal rights eventually, but is it possible that you are in too great of a religious hurry? It has taken Christianity almost 2000 years to accomplish what it has. The teachings of Christ take time to come to earth." All that is said here grows out of a tragic misconception of time. It is the strangely irrational notion that there is something in the very flow of time that will inevitably cure all ills. Actually time is neutral. It can be used either destructively or constructively. I am coming to feel that the people of ill will will have used time much more effectively than the people of good will. We will have to repent in this generation not merely for the vitriolic words and actions of the bad people, but for the appalling silence of the good people. We must come to see that human progress never rolls in on wheels of inevitability. It comes through the tireless efforts and persistent work of men willing to be co-workers with God, and without this hard work time itself becomes an ally of the forces of social stagnation.

We must use time creatively, and forever realize that the time is always ripe to do right. Now is the time to make real the promise of democracy, and transform our pending national elegy into a creative psalm of brotherhood. Now is the time to lift our national policy from the quicksand of racial injustice to the solid rock of human dignity.

You spoke of our activity in Birmingham as extreme. At first I was rather disappointed that fellow clergymen would see my nonviolent efforts as those of the extremist. I started thinking about the fact that I stand in the middle of two opposing forces in the Negro community. One is a force of complacency made up of Negroes who, as a result of long years of oppression, have been so completely drained of self-respect and a sense of "somebodiness" that they have adjusted to segregation, and of a few Negroes in the middle class who, because of a degree of academic and economic security, and because at points they profit by segregation, have unconsciously become insensitive to the problems of the masses. The other force is one of bitterness and hatred and comes perilously close to advocating violence. It is expressed in the various black nationalist groups that are springing up over the nation, the largest and best known being Elijah Muhammad's Muslim movement. This movement is nourished by the contemporary frustration over the continued existence of racial discrimination. It is made up of people who have lost faith in America, who have absolutely repudiated Christianity, and who have concluded that the white man is an incurable "devil." I have tried to stand between these two forces saying that we need not follow the "do-nothingism" of the complacent or the hatred and despair of the black nationalist. There is the more excellent way of love and nonviolent protest. I'm grateful to God that, through the Negro church, the dimension of nonviolence entered our struggle. If this philosophy had not emerged I am convinced that by now many streets of the South would be flowing with floods of blood. And I am further convinced that if our white brothers dismiss us as "rabble rousers" and "outside agitators"—those of us who are working through the channels of nonviolent direct action—and refuse to support our nonviolent efforts, millions of Negroes, out of frustration and despair, will seek solace and security in black nationalist ideologies, a development that will lead inevitably to a frightening racial nightmare.

Oppressed people cannot remain oppressed forever. The urge for freedom will eventually come. This is what has happened to the American Negro. Something within has reminded him of his birthright of freedom; something without has reminded him that he can gain it. Consciously and unconsciously, he has been swept in by what the Germans call the *Zeitgeist,* and with his black brothers of Africa, and his brown and yellow brothers of Asia, South America, and the Caribbean, he is moving with a sense of cosmic urgency toward the promised land of racial justice. Recognizing this vital urge that has engulfed the Negro community, one should readily understand public demonstrations. The Negro has many pent-up resentments and latent frustrations. He has to get them out. So let him march sometime; let him have his prayer pilgrimages to the city hall; understand why he must have sit-ins and freedom rides. If his repressed emotions do not come out in these nonviolent ways, they will come out in ominous expressions of violence. This is not a threat; it is a fact of history. So I have not said to my people, "Get rid of your discontent." But I have tried to say that this normal and healthy discontent can be channeled through the creative outlet of nonviolent direct action. Now this approach is being dismissed as extremist. I must admit that I was initially disappointed in being so categorized.

But as I continued to think about the matter I gradually gained a bit of satisfaction from being considered an extremist. Was not Jesus an extremist in love? "Love your enemies, bless them that curse you, pray for them that despitefully use you." Was not Amos an extremist for justice—"Let justice roll down like waters and righteousness like a mighty stream." Was not Paul an extremist for the gospel of Jesus Christ—"I bear in my body the marks of the Lord Jesus." Was not Martin Luther an extremist—"Here I stand; I can do none other so help me God." Was not John Bunyan an extremist—"I will stay in jail to the end of my days before I make a butchery of my conscience." Was not Abraham Lincoln an extremist—"This nation cannot survive half slave and half free." Was not Thomas Jefferson an extremist—"We hold these truths to be self-evident; that all men were created equal." So the question is not whether we will be extremist but what kind of extremist will we be. Will we be extremists for hate or will we be extremists for love? Will we be extremists for the preservation of injustice—or will we be extremists for the cause of justice? In that dramatic scene on Calvary's hill three men were crucified. We must never forget that all three were crucified for the same crime—the crime of extremism. Two were extremists for immorality, and thus fell below their environment. The other, Jesus Christ, was an extremist for love, truth, and goodness, and thereby rose above His environment. So, after all, maybe the South, the nation, and the world are in dire need of creative extremists.

I had hoped that the white moderate would see this. Maybe I was too optimistic. Maybe I expected too much. I guess I should have realized that few members of a race that has oppressed another race can understand or appreciate the deep groans and passionate yearnings of those that have been oppressed, and still fewer have the vision to see that injustice must be rooted out by strong, persistent, and determined action. I am thankful, however, that some of our white brothers have grasped the meaning of this social revolution and committed themselves to it. They are still all too small in quantity, but they are big in quality. Some like Ralph McGill, Lillian Smith, Harry Golden, and James Dabbs have written about our struggle in eloquent, prophetic, and understanding terms. Others have marched with us down nameless streets of the South. They have languished in filthy, roach-infested jails, suffering the abuse and brutality of angry policemen who see them as "dirty nigger lovers." They, unlike so many of their moderate brothers and sisters, have recognized the urgency of the moment and sensed the need for powerful "action" antidotes to combat the disease of segregation.

Let me rush on to mention my other disappointment. I have been so greatly disappointed with the white Church and its leadership. Of course there are some notable exceptions. I am not unmindful of the fact that each of you has taken some significant stands on this issue. I commend you, Rev. Stallings, for your Christian stand on this past Sunday, in welcoming Negroes to your worship service on a non-segregated basis. I commend the Catholic leaders of this state for integrating Springhill College several years ago.

But despite these notable exceptions I must honestly reiterate that I have been disappointed with the Church. I do not say that as one of those negative critics who can always find something wrong with the Church. I say it as a minister of the gospel, who loves the Church; who was nurtured in its bosom; who has been sustained by its spiritual blessings and who will remain true to it as long as the cord of life shall lengthen.

I had the strange feeling when I was suddenly catapulted into the leadership of the bus protest in Montgomery several years ago that we would have the support of the white Church. I felt that the white ministers, priests, and rabbis of the South would be some of our strongest allies. Instead, some have been outright opponents, refusing to understand the freedom movement and misrepresenting its leaders; all too many others have been more cautious than courageous and have remained silent behind the anesthetizing security of stained glass windows.

In spite of my shattered dreams of the past, I came to Birmingham with the hope that the white religious leadership of this community would see the justice of our cause and, with deep moral concern, serve as the channel through which our just grievances could get to the power structure. I had hoped that each of you would understand. But again I have been disappointed.

I have heard numerous religious leaders of the South call upon their worshippers to comply with a desegregation decision because it is the law, but I have longed to hear white ministers say follow this decree because integration is morally right and the Negro is your brother. In the midst of blatant injustices inflicted upon the Negro, I have watched white churches stand on the sideline and merely mouth pious irrelevancies and sanctimonious trivialities. In the midst of a mighty struggle to rid our nation of racial and economic injustice, I have heard so many ministers say, "Those are social issues with which the Gospel has no real concern," and I have watched so many churches commit themselves to a completely other-worldly religion which made a strange distinction between body and soul, the sacred and the secular.

So here we are moving toward the exit of the twentieth century with a religious community largely adjusted to the status quo, standing as a taillight behind other community agencies rather than a headlight leading men to higher levels of justice.

I have travelled the length and breadth of Alabama, Mississippi, and all the other Southern states. On sweltering summer days and crisp autumn mornings I have looked at her beautiful churches with their spires pointing heavenward. I have beheld the impressive outlay of her massive religious education buildings. Over and over again I have found myself asking: "Who worships here? Who is their God? Where were their voices when the lips of Governor Barnett dripped with words of interposition and nullification? Where were they when Governor Wallace gave the clarion call for defiance and hatred? Where were their voices of support when tired, bruised, and weary Negro men and women decided to rise from the dark dungeons of complacency to the bright hills of creative protest?"

Yes, these questions are still in my mind. In deep disappointment, I have wept over the laxity of the Church. But be assured that my tears have been tears of love. There can be no deep disappointment where there is not deep love. Yes, I love the Church; I love her sacred walls. How could I do otherwise? I am in the rather unique position of being the son, the grandson, and the great grandson of preachers. Yes, I see the Church as the body of Christ. But, oh! How we have blemished and scarred that body through social neglect and fear of being nonconformist.

There was a time when the Church was very powerful. It was during that period when the early Christians rejoiced when they were deemed worthy to suffer for what they believed. In those days the Church was not merely a thermometer that recorded the ideas and principles of popular opinion; it was a thermostat that transformed the mores of society. Wherever the early Christians entered a town the power structure got disturbed and immediately sought to convict them for being "disturbers of the peace" and "outside agitators." But they went on with the conviction that they were a "colony of heaven" and had to obey God rather than man. They were small in number but big in commitment. They were too God-intoxicated to be "astronomically intimidated." They brought an end to such ancient evils as infanticide and gladiatorial contest.

Things are different now. The contemporary Church is so often a weak, ineffectual voice with an uncertain sound. It is so often the arch-supporter of the status quo. Far from being disturbed by the presence of the Church, the power structure of the average community is consoled by the Church's silent and often vocal sanction of things as they are.

But the judgment of God is upon the Church as never before. If the Church of today does not recapture the sacrificial spirit of the early Church, it will lose its authentic ring, forfeit the loyalty of millions, and be dismissed as an irrelevant social club with no meaning for the twentieth century. I am meeting young people every day whose disappointment with the Church has risen to outright disgust.

Maybe again I have been too optimistic. Is organized religion too inextricably bound to the status quo to save our nation and the world? Maybe I must turn my faith to the inner spiritual Church, the church within the Church, as the true *ecclesia* and the hope of the world. But again I am thankful to God that some noble souls from the ranks of organized religion have broken loose from the paralyzing chains of conformity and joined us as active partners in the struggle for freedom. They have left their secure congregations and walked the streets of Albany, Georgia, with us. They have gone through the highways of the South on torturous rides for freedom. Yes, they have gone to jail with us. Some have been kicked out of their churches and lost the support of their bishops and fellow ministers. But they have gone with the faith that right defeated is stronger than evil triumphant. These men have been the leaven in the lump of the race. Their witness has been the spiritual salt that has preserved the true meaning of the gospel in these troubled times. They have carved a tunnel of hope through the dark mountain of disappointment.

I hope the Church as a whole will meet the challenge of this decisive hour. But even if the Church does not come to the aid of justice, I have no despair about the future. I have no fear about the outcome of our struggle in Birmingham, even if our motives are presently misunderstood. We will reach the goal of freedom in Birmingham and all over the nation, because the goal of America is freedom. Abused and scorned though we may be, our destiny is tied up with the destiny of America. Before the Pilgrims landed at Plymouth, we were here. Before the pen of Jefferson etched across the pages of history the majestic words of the Declaration of Independence, we were here. For more than two centuries our foreparents labored in this country without wages; they made cotton "king"; and they built the homes of their masters in the midst of brutal injustice and shameful humiliation—and yet out of a bottomless vitality they continued to thrive and develop. If the inexpressible cruelties of slavery could not stop us, the opposition we now face will surely fail. We will win our freedom because the sacred heritage of our nation and the eternal will of God are embodied in our echoing demands.

I must close now. But before closing I am impelled to mention one other point in your statement that troubled me profoundly. You warmly commended the Birmingham police force for keeping "order" and "preventing violence." I don't believe you would have so warmly commended the police force if you had seen its angry violent dogs literally biting six unarmed, nonviolent Negroes. I don't believe you would so quickly commend the policemen if you would observe their ugly and inhuman treatment of Negroes here in the city jail; if you would watch them push and curse old Negro women and young Negro girls; if you would see them slap and kick old Negro men and young Negro boys; if you will observe them, as they did on two occasions, refuse to give us food because we wanted to sing our grace together. I'm sorry that I can't join you in your praise for the police department.

It is true that they have been rather disciplined in their public handling of the demonstrators. In this sense they have been rather publicly "nonviolent." But for what purpose? To preserve the evil system of segregation. Over the last few years I have consistently preached that nonviolence demands that the means we use must be as pure as the ends we seek. So I have tried to make it clear that it is wrong to use immoral means to attain moral ends. But now I must affirm that it is just as wrong, or even more so, to use moral means to preserve immoral ends. Maybe Mr. Connor and his policemen have been rather publicly nonviolent, as Chief Prichett was in Albany, Georgia, but they have used the moral means of nonviolence to maintain the immoral end of flagrant racial injustice. T. S. Eliot has said that there is no greater treason than to do the right deed for the wrong reason.

I wish you had commended the Negro sit-inners and demonstrators of Birmingham for their sublime courage, their willingness to suffer, and their amazing discipline in the midst of the most inhuman provocation. One day the South will recognize its real heroes. They will be the James Merediths, courageously and with a majestic sense of purpose, facing jeering and hostile mobs and the agonizing loneliness that characterizes the life of the pioneer. They will be old, oppressed, battered Negro women, symbolized in a seventy-two-year-old woman of Montgomery, Alabama, who rose up with a sense of dignity and with her people decided not to ride the segregated buses, and responded to one who inquired about her tiredness with ungrammatical profundity: "My feets is tired, but my soul is rested." They will be young high school and college students, young ministers of the gospel and a host of the elders, courageously and nonviolently sitting in at lunch counters and willingly going to jail for conscience sake. One day the South will know that when these disinherited children of God sat down at lunch counters they were in reality standing up for the best in the American dream and the most sacred values in our Judeo-Christian heritage, and thus carrying our whole nation back to great wells of democracy which were dug deep by the founding fathers in the formulation of the Constitution and the Declaration of Independence.

Never before have I written a letter this long (or should I say a book?). I'm afraid that it is much too long to take your precious time. I can assure you that it would have been much shorter if I had been writing from a comfortable desk, but what else is there to do when you are alone for days in the dull monotony of a narrow jail cell other than write long letters, think strange thoughts, and pray long prayers?

If I have said anything in this letter that is an overstatement of the truth and is indicative of an unreasonable impatience, I beg you to forgive me. If I have said anything in this letter that is an understatement of the truth and is indicative of my having a patience that makes me patient with anything less than brotherhood, I beg God to forgive me.

I hope this letter finds you strong in the faith. I also hope that circumstances will soon make it possible for me to meet each of you, not as an integrationist or a civil rights leader, but as a fellow clergyman and a Christian brother. Let us all hope that the dark clouds of racial prejudice will soon pass away and the deep fog of misunderstanding will be lifted from our fear-drenched communities and in some not too distant tomorrow the radiant stars of love and brotherhood will shine over our great nation with all of their scintillating beauty.

Yours for the cause of Peace and Brotherhood

MARTIN LUTHER KING, JR.

9

*A Correspondence**

Emil Brunner/Karl Barth

An Open Letter to Karl Barth

Many will no doubt have read your report on Hungary with as great an interest as I have done. But not a few, including some of your own theological associates, have been extremely surprised by your attitude to the political problems of the church under Soviet rule. Those who were familiar with the pronouncements on current events which you have issued since the end of the war were aware that your attitude to the great Communist power in the East was, if not friendly, at any rate emphatically sympathetic, and deliberately avoided any harsh outright rejection of Communist pretensions. I myself have only been able to interpret your approach as an after-effect of the satisfaction you felt at the overpowering of the brown monster in which Communist Russia played such a leading part. I had hoped that this mildness would automatically disappear and give way to a more fundamental judgment as soon as the true character of that power had emerged more clearly. I imagined you would undergo the same change of outlook as Reinhold Niebuhr, who only two years ago was expressing doubts about my fundamental rejection of Communist totalitarianism at an important ecumenical conference, but who has since joined the absolute opponents of Communism, particularly since seeing the monster at close quarters in Berlin. What I cannot understand—and it is this that prompts me to write an open letter to you—is why a similar change has not occurred in your attitude—even after the recent events in Prague.

Not only after the end of the war and during the last two years, but

---

*Published in *Against the Stream* by Karl Barth (1954) 106–18.

even now, you are passing on the watchword that the church must not allow itself to be dragged into a clear-cut, fundamental opposition to "Communism." You praise the Reformed Hungarians for not "sharing that nervousness about the Russians, the peoples' democracies and the whole problem of Eastern Europe which some people in our own country apparently regard as inevitable." You evidently agree with your pupil Hermann Diem that in its first encounter with the "Communism" of the East the Evangelical church should not reject it out of hand but wait and see, and be ready to cooperate. I don't know if you even approve of the attitude of your friend Hromadka in Prague, who belongs to the Communist Action Committee and who, although he prophesied only a short time ago in England that there would be no *coup d'état* in Prague, since Czech Communism was different from Russian Communism, was, when the crisis came, ready to cooperate.

All this is inexplicable to those who can see no fundamental difference between Communist and any other brand of totalitarianism, for example, Nazism. Naturally we who have taken this line for many years realize that the origins and original motivation of Russian Communism were quite different from those of Nazism. We know too that certain postulates of social justice appear to be fulfilled in Communist totalitarianism. In brief, we know that the red variety of totalitarianism is different from the brown.

The question we want to ask you, however—and when I say "we" I mean not only the Swiss, but also many of your theological friends in Germany, Britain and America—is whether, whatever the differences between the several varieties, totalitarianism as such is a quantity to which the Christian church can only issue an absolute, unmistakable and passionate No!, just as you said No! to Hitlerism and summoned the church to say an absolute No! Let me make a few observations to establish and explain the question:

1. I was always struck, and probably others were too, by the fact that even at the height of your struggle against Nazism you always evaded the problem of totalitarianism. Passionate and absolute as was your hostility to that incarnation of social injustice, if I am not mistaken, you hardly ever attacked the fundamental illegality and inhumanity inherent in the very nature of totalitarianism as such. This may have struck me more than others, since as far back as the spring of 1934 I became involved in a sharp exchange with some German theologians at an ecumenical conference in Paris because

they refused to swallow my thesis that the totalitarian state is *eo ipso* an unjust, inhuman and godless state. Since then I have repeatedly defended that position, and was therefore never able wholly to agree with the thesis you put forward in Wipkingen in 1938, that National Socialism was "the" political problem of the church in our time, wholeheartedly as I agreed with you that it was the primary and most urgent problem from a purely political and military point of view.

2. I have been equally struck by the fact that in your utterances and those of your closest friends the problem of the totalitarian state is displaced by two other problems, which I can only regard as concealing the real problem. You talk about "the problem of East and West" and the problem of "Communism."

If the only issue was a "problem of East and West" the church would certainly do well not to join too ostentatiously in the conversations of the politicians. For "East and West" is undoubtedly not a problem in which the church as such has anything authoritative to say. But what one must not forget is that there are nations in Eastern Europe today which have been violated and regard themselves as having been violated by a political despotism in the same way as non-German nations did under Hitler. Nazism did not become an "Eastern" problem because Hitler occupied large territories in Eastern Europe. Because a political system subjugates and controls by means of puppet governments the peoples of Russia, the Baltic, Poland and the Balkans, the conflict today has certainly not become one between East and West. That would be the case only if the nations involved had given their consent to the Communist system, and if such consent could be explained on the grounds of traditional modes of thinking in Eastern Europe. Today everyone with eyes to see knows that that is not so. We churchmen really ought not to associate ourselves with such a camouflaging of the truth.

3. The other shift of emphasis is rather better founded, though no less dangerous. People—including yourself—talk simply about the "Communism" which the church should not reject outright. Certainly the Christian who believes in the communion of saints and celebrates Holy Communion, cannot be against "Communism" as such. Among the many possible forms of Communism there are some with thoroughly Christian potentialities. One can indeed argue, as I have often done, that the system that calls itself Communism today would not have become possible if the church had been more communistic on the lines of the communism we find in the Acts of the Apostles which is inherent in the very nature of the Christian society.

What we are dealing with today, however, is a manifestation of the totalitarian state, a totalitarian Communism. This so-called Communism is the logical consequence of totalitarianism. If Hitler did not get as far as total nationalization, total political and military control until the last years of the war, it only shows what an amateur he was. The "fully matured," the consistent totalitarian state must be "communistic," since one of its essential foundations is the subjugation to the state of the whole of life and the whole of man. And the nationalization of the whole economic life of the country is the indispensable first step towards the totalitarian state. The question which confronts the church today is therefore not whether or not it should adopt a fundamentally negative attitude towards "Communism," but whether it can say anything but a passionately fundamental No to the totalitarian state which, to be consistent, must also be communistic.

4. You justify the rejection of a fundamentally negative answer to "Communism" by referring to the social injustice of which there is certainly no lack in the nations of the West. The alternative as it is usually put sounds more imposing: Communism or Capitalism? Of course, the church cannot and should not deny that there is a great deal of scandalous social injustice in the West. Of course it must fight against all social wrongs with the utmost earnestness and passion. Whether it does well to adopt the slogan of "capitalism" as the embodiment of social evil will depend on whether it knows what it means by capitalism. If it only means an economy which is not nationalized, I would resist the war cry vigorously. The crucial point, however, is that we must never forget that in the countries not under totalitarian control it is still possible to fight against social injustice, that the fight is being waged and has already achieved a great deal, though nothing like enough.

5. If I am correctly informed, you are still a Socialist. However you interpret the Socialism in which you believe—the English interpretation, for example, is very different from that of our "socialist" press, and the current German version is quite different from the one in fashion there twenty years ago—one thing cannot be denied: Socialism is engaged in a life and death struggle against "Communism" because and insofar as it is fundamentally and passionately anti-totalitarian. Is it therefore a good thing that this anti-totalitarian Socialism should be attacked in the rear—by churchmen of all people—in its defensive fight against totalitarian Communism? This is the effect of your statement that the well-advised Christian cannot be anti-Communist. Do you mean that Christians must not participate

in the common struggle which the bourgeoisie and Socialism are waging against totalitarian Communism? I believe that would amount to a denial of principles which the Christian must never deny. Why not? Well, what is at stake in the struggle against totalitarianism? What is totalitarianism?

6. The totalitarian state is based on, is in fact identical with, the denial of those rights of the person vis-à-vis the state which are usually called human rights. That was the situation in Hitler's state, and it is the same now in the Communist totalitarian state. The individual has no original rights conferred on him as a creature of God. Only the state can establish rights, and the individual only has the rights the state gives him and can take away from him at any time.

The totalitarian state is therefore a state of basic injustice. It is therefore also fundamentally inhuman and a fundamental denial of personal dignity. It is therefore intrinsically godless even though it may, like the Nazi state, tolerate the church within certain narrow limits, or like Communist totalitarianism, for reasons of expediency keep its openly declared war on religion within certain bounds which just make it possible for the church to exist.

The totalitarian state is intrinsically atheistic and anti-theistic since, by definition, it claims the total allegiance of man. From this intrinsic nature of totalitarianism all the familiar, ghastly phenomena have resulted which we got to know from the Russian state from 1917 to 1948, and from the Nazi state from 1933 to 1945: the G.P.U. and the Gestapo; the concentration camp without legal proceedings; the slave labor of millions; the utter uncertainty of the law, and so on. My question is: can the church possibly say anything but a passionate and absolute No to totalitarianism? Must it not take its stand just as definitely against "Communism," that is, against the consistently totalitarian state as against the amateurish Nazi state?

7. You assert that the Communist state realizes certain social postulates which the Christian cannot oppose, but must on the contrary welcome. We heard exactly the same argument in the Hitler state—how often they tried to hoodwink us with the marvelous social achievements of the Nazi regime—things which it was impossible flatly to deny and which persuaded the naive to believe that, in spite of all the horrors, "at bottom" National Socialism was a good thing. It cannot be denied that the Communist state has achieved and is achieving all kinds of valuable things—how else could it continue to exist at all? But as Christians we surely know it is always the devil's way to mix elements of truth in the system of lies and to endue a

system of injustice with certain splendid appearances of justice. Are we no longer to fight the system of injustice, which is what the totalitarian state is fundamentally, because it also contains a number of valuable achievements? The dividing up of large estates was certainly a long overdue measure, in the interests of a healthy economy and a free peasantry. And it is also open to debate how far the nationalizing of certain branches of economic life is not in the interest of justice and the common weal. Regarding the last point, I am more skeptical than my Socialist friends; but it is a matter that is certainly worth discussing amongst Christians. What is not open to discussion, however, is whether, because of measures such as these, which may be justified in themselves, the system of injustice and inhumanity which totalitarianism is, may be considered a feasible system for Christians.

8. Your friend Hromadka defends the strange view that Communism—meaning the totalitarian Communism which is the only variety we are concerned with today—is a historical necessity, since democracy has proved its inability to survive: therefore the Christian church must welcome Communism. We heard just the same argument in Switzerland during the worst years of the Hitler regime. I regard it as an utterly dangerous aberration of which a Protestant theologian ought to be thoroughly ashamed. A doubtful piece of historical determinism, shaky in relation to facts and principles alike, is used to confer the status of a normative principle on what amounts to an abdication of ethics and a surrender to the brute force of reality. Since when has the Christian capitulated in the face of "historical necessities"? Certainly there are situations in which the Christian or the church is powerless to do anything, in which they cannot prevent disasters, in which they cannot redress even the most flagrant injustice, in which they may not even be able to protest publicly without endangering their very existence. All the more reason, surely, why the church should beware of giving an ethical sanction to something it is powerless to prevent—but that is precisely what Hromadka is doing. What will he, what will his friends have to say for themselves when this totalitarian system that has been forced on their people collapses and is brought to judgment, as the Nazi system was brought to judgment in the Nuremberg Trials? They will stand convicted as collaborators, who not merely cooperated with the power of tyranny and injustice but even set themselves up as its champions!

9. There is one final argument which we find in your utterances and those of your friends: this fundamental attack on "Communism" is something the Catholic church is engaged in—therefore

we Protestants should not join in. I do not feel called upon to defend Catholic politics. I know perfectly well how much the Catholics always pursue their own power-political ends, how much, especially in Hungary, the Catholic church is defending its former privileges in its struggle against Communism. But when the Catholic church declares that the totalitarian state, red or brown, is irreconcilable with the Christian faith, why should the Evangelical church have to stand aside merely because the truth is spoken by the Catholic church? Did not Catholics and Protestants stand together in the struggle against the Hitler regime, and did you yourself not rejoice in the brave utterances of individual Catholic leaders and heartily agree with them when they condemned the totalitarian state passionately and unconditionally? A doctrine does not become false simply because it is expressed by the Catholic church even if we always have good reason to reserve to ourselves the right to deviate from the Catholics and interpret and justify the doctrine more closely.

10. One further word about Hungary. I have not visited post-war Hungary, but I am fairly well-informed about what is going on, and I know how many different interpretations of the situation are current there. I know that very many good members of the Reformed church view with the utmost consternation these new collaborationist slogans, these tendencies toward a "positive evaluation" which are inspired by Pétain-Tildy, himself a member of the Reformed church. The Reformed collaborators, even the Reformed fellow-travelers, will have to atone bitterly one day, I was told by someone who has suffered severely under the Communists. And even now many are turning away disillusioned from these members of the Reformed church, because they feel they are betraying the cause of freedom, human rights, justice, and humanity.

I simply cannot grasp why you, of all people, who condemned so severely even a semblance of collaborationism on the part of the church under Hitler, should now be making yourself the spokesman of those who condemn not merely outward but even inward spiritual resistance, and why you should deride as "nervousness" what is really a horror-struck revulsion from a truly diabolical system of injustice and inhumanity; why you, who were only recently condemning in the most unsparing terms those Germans who withdrew to a purely inward line in the struggle against Hitlerism, and maintained that the Christian duty was simply to proclaim the Word of God under whatever political system, why you now suddenly advocate the very same line and commend the theologians in Hungary who "are occupied not with the rights and wrongs of their present government but simply with the positive tasks of their own church." Have you now returned, after a fifteen years' intermezzo of theologically political activism, to that attitude of passive unconcern in which, in the first number of *Theologische Existenz heute*, you summoned the church to apply itself simply to its task of preaching the gospel, "as if nothing had happened"?

I have felt bound to submit this question to you in my own name and in that of many of those who listen to you who are equally disturbed. Mindful of the great influence of whatever you say, you will surely regard it as a duty to give the question a clear answer.

Your EMIL BRUNNER

Karl Barth's Reply

Dear Emil Brunner,

You do not seem to understand. At the moment I am not rousing the church to oppose Communism and to witness against it, in the same way as I did between 1933 and 1945 in the case of National Socialism; you demand a "clear reply" to the question of how this is to be construed. I will come straight to the point.

Let us begin with a general statement. A certain binding spiritual and theological viewpoint in accordance with its creed is demanded of the church in the political realm in certain times of need, that is, when it is called upon to vindicate its faith in the carrying out of its duty according to God's Word, or when it is called upon to give an explanation regarding a definite occurrence. The church must not concern itself eternally with various "isms" and systems, but with historical realities as seen in the light of the Word of God and of the Faith. Its obligations lie, not in the direction of any fulfilling of the law of nature, but toward its living Lord. Therefore, the church never thinks, speaks or acts "on principle." Rather it judges spiritually and by individual cases. For that reason it rejects every attempt to systematize political history and its own part in that history. Therefore, it preserves the freedom to judge each new event afresh. If yesterday it traveled along one path, it is not bound to keep to the same path today. If yesterday it spoke from its position of responsibility, then today it should be silent if in this position it considers silence to be the better course. The unity and continuity of theology will best be preserved if the church does not let itself be discouraged from being up-to-date theologically.

I ask this question: Was it not true that in the years after 1933 up till the end of the war there really was this need? The Central and Western European peoples—first Germany, then the others—had succumbed to Hitler's spell. He had become a spiritual and, almost everywhere, a political source of temptation. He had English, French, and American admirers. Did not even Churchill have a few friendly words to say for him? And in Switzerland there were more than two hundred sympathizers, there was a Rudolf Grob, there were innumerable people who were impressed and influenced, though also very many who were frightened and despondent. One of the most important aims of our political authorities was to preserve correct and friendly relations with our powerful neighbor. In the Swiss Zofinger Society there was a serious discussion as to whether it was not time to subject our democratic system, established in 1848 (which event we are triumphantly celebrating today) to a thorough revision. Of the state of the press one can read in the edifying book by Karl Weber, *Switzerland in the War of Nerves*. How great were the cares of our military directors can be seen from the account of our General, and from the fine book by Lt.-Col. Barbey about the five years he spent in the General's entourage. It was at that time that I made my various attempts to make the church ready for action against the temptations of National Socialism, in Germany obviously spiritual, in Switzerland obviously political. At that time it had to warn men against tempters, to recall those who had strayed, to rouse the careless, to "confirm the feeble knees," to comfort sorrowing hearts.

Whether the essence of National Socialism consisted in its "totalitarianism" or, according to other views, in its "nihilism," or again in its barbarism, or anti-Semitism, or whether it was a final, concluding outburst of the militarism which had taken hold on Germany like a madness since 1870—what made it interesting from the Christian point of view was that it was a spell which notoriously revealed its power to overwhelm our souls, to persuade us to believe in its lies and to join in its evil-doings. It could and would take us captive with "strong mail of craft and power." We were hypnotized by it as a rabbit by a giant snake. We were in danger of bringing, first incense, and then the complete sacrifice to it as to a false god. That ought not to have been done. We had to object with all our protestantism as though against *the* evil. It was not a matter of declaiming against some mischief, distant and easily seen through. It was a matter of life and death, of resistance against a godlessness which was in fact attacking body and soul, and was therefore effectively masked to many thousands of Christian eyes. For that very reason I spoke then and was not silent. For that very reason I could not forgive the collaborators, least of all those among them who were cultured, decent, and well-meaning. In that way I consider that I acted as befits a churchman.

Now a second question: Is it not true that today there is again a state of emergency, this time in the shape of Communism? Has history already repeated itself, in that today we only need to take the remedy (which at that time took long enough to learn) from out of our pockets and to make immediate use of it? In the last few years I have become acquainted with Western Germany and also with the non-Russian sectors of Berlin. Fear, distrust, and hatred for the "Eastern monster," as you call it, I met there in abundance, but apart from the German Communists I met no man of whom I received the impression (as one did with almost everybody in 1933) that he felt that this "monster" was a vexation, a temptation, an enticement, or that he was in danger of liking it or of condoning its deeds and of cooperating with it. On the contrary, it was quite clear to everyone, and it was universally agreed, that for many reasons there was nothing in it. Is the situation any different here in Switzerland? in France, England or America? Are we not all convinced, whether we have read *I Chose Freedom* or not, that we cannot consider the way of life of the people in Soviet territory and in the Soviet-controlled "peoples' democracies" to be worthy, acceptable, or of advantage to us, because it does not conform to our standards of justice and freedom? Who can contradict this? A few Western European Communists! Yet are we in danger of letting ourselves be overwhelmed by this power merely on account of the existence and the activities of these latter? Is there not freedom for every man—and who would not take advantage of this freedom?—to vent his anger against this "monster" to his heart's content, and again and again to bring to light its evils as "thoroughly" and as "passionately" as he wishes? Anyone who would like from me a political disclaimer of its system and its methods may have it at once. However, what is given cheaply can be had cheaply. Surely it would cost no one anything—not even a little thought—certainly nothing more, to add his bundle of faggots to the bonfire? I cannot admit that this is a repetition of the situation and of the tasks during the years of 1933 to 1945. For I cannot admit that it is the duty of Christians or of the church to give theological backing to what every citizen can, with much shaking of his head, read in his daily paper and what is so admirably expressed by Mr. Truman and by the pope. Has the "East" or whatever we may call it, really such a hold over us that we must needs oppose it with our last breath when the last but one would suffice? No, when the church witnesses it moves in fear and trembling, not with the stream but against it. Today it certainly has no cause to move against the stream and thus to witness to Communism because it could never be worthy of it, either in its Marxist or its imperialist, or let us say, in its Asiatic aspects. Must the church then move with the stream and thus side with America and the Vatican, merely because somewhere in the textbooks of its professors—ever since 1934—it has rightly been said that "totalitarianism" is a dreadful thing? Where is the spiritual danger and need which the church would meet if it witnessed to this truth, where is its commission to do so? Whom would it teach, enlighten, rouse, set on the right path, comfort, and lead to repentance and a new way of life? Surely not the "Christian" peoples of the West, nor the Americans! Are they not already sure enough of the justice of their cause against Russia without this truth and our Christian support? Surely not the poor Russians and even the poor Communists? For how should they be able to understand what the Western church, which in the old days and even today has accepted so much "totalitarianism" and has cooperated with it without witnessing against it, claims to have against their church? Surely not the Christian churches behind the Iron Curtain? In their struggle with the "monster" it would be no help at all to them if we were to proclaim those well-known truths as energetically as possible, since we are not asked for them anyway, nor would they cost us anything. As it is not possible to give satisfactory answers to these questions, I am of the opinion that the church today—contrary to its action between 1933 and 1945—ought to stand quietly aloof from the present conflict and not let off all its guns before it is necessary but wait calmly to see whether and in what sense the situation will grow serious again and call for speech. If a definite spiritual crisis were again to develop as it did during the years 1933–45— though we do not yet know from what direction it is likely to come— then a concrete answer would be demanded from us, for which we ourselves should have to pay: then it would be obvious against whom and for whom we should have to witness, and whether and how far we should be prepared for this new emergency. Then something would be at stake other than these eternal truths which you wish me to proclaim. According to my view, we shall then profit more from the first article of the Declaration of Barmen than from your knowledge of the objectionableness of "totalitarianism."

But, however that may be, with this problem in view I met responsible members of the Reformed church in Hungary and thought that I could encourage them in their attempt to walk along the narrow path midway between Moscow and Rome. I did not take a ruler with me to draw this dividing line, so I could not leave one behind for their use. Their past history, their present situation, and their task do not resemble ours, nor those of the Evangelical church in Germany which is joining in the battle. They have come to an agreement with the new regime and are directing all their energies toward the positive tasks of their church, and this is not the same as what the central parties, which you esteem so highly, or even the "German Christians," are doing in the battle for the church in Germany. Incidentally, it is a legend without historical foundation that in 1933 I recommended "passive resistance" when I urged the Germans to fulfil their duties of Christian witness "as though nothing had happened," that is, ignoring Adolf Hitler's alleged divine revelation. If they had consequently done so, they would have built up against National Socialism a political factor of the first order.

For Hungary, though not only for this country, everything depends on whether the church, not bound to abstract principles but to its living Lord, will seek and find its own way and also learn to choose freely the time for speech and the time for silence and all the various other times mentioned in Ecclesiastes, chapter 3, without thereby becoming confused by any law other than that of the gospel.

Your KARL BARTH

Basel
June 6th, 1948

Bibliography

Ames, James Barr. "Law and Morals." *Harvard Law Review* 22 (1908) 97–113.

Arneson, Richard. "Mill versus Paternalism." *Ethics* 90 (1980) 470–89.

Atiyah, P. S. *Promises, Morals, and Law.* Oxford: Clarendon Press, 1981.

Ball, Milner A. *The Promise of American Law: A Theological, Humanistic View of Legal Process.* Athens: University of Georgia Press, 1981.

Beauchamp, Tom L. "Paternalism and Biobehavioral Control." *Monist* 60 (1977) 62–80.

Bedau, Hugo Adam, ed. *Civil Disobedience: Theory and Practice.* New York: Pegasus, 1969.

Berman, Harold. *Law and Revolution: The Formation of the Western Legal Tradition.* Cambridge, Mass.: Harvard University Press, 1983.

Beyleveld, Deryck, and Roger Brownsword. "Law as a Moral Judgment vs. Law as the Rules of the Powerful." *American Journal of Jurisprudence* 28 (1983) 79–117.

_____. "The Practical Difference Between Natural Law Theory and Legal Positivism." *Oxford Journal of Legal Studies* 5 (1985) 1–32.

Cahn, Edmund. *The Moral Decision: Right and Wrong in the Light of American Law.* Bloomington, Ind.: Indiana University Press, 1955.

Childress, James F. *Civil Disobedience and Political Obligation.* New Haven: Yale University Press, 1971.

_____. "Paternalism and Health Care." In *Medical Responsibility,* edited by Wade L. Robison and Michael S. Pritchard, 15–28. Clifton, N.J.: Humana Press, 1979.

Cohen, Marshall. "Civil Disobedience in a Constitutional Democracy." *Massachusetts Review* 10 (1969) 211–26.

Coleman, Jules. "Legal Duty and Moral Argument." *Social Theory and Practice* 5 (1979) 377–407.

Cornell, Drucilla. "Toward a Modern/Postmodern Reconstruction of Ethics." *University of Pennsylvania Law Review* 133 (1985) 291–380.

Cranor, Carl F. "Legal Moralism Reconsidered." *Ethics* 89 (1979) 147–64.

Cranston, Maurice. "Are There Any Human Rights?" *Daedalus* 112 (Fall 1983) 1–17.

Dworkin, Ronald. *Taking Rights Seriously.* Cambridge, Mass.: Harvard University Press, 1977.

———. *A Matter of Principle.* Cambridge, Mass.: Harvard University Press, 1985.

"Ethics and Regulations" [discussion and papers]. *Hastings Center Report* 10 (February 1980) 25–41.

Ellin, Joseph. "Fidelity to Law." *Soundings* 51 (1968) 401–31.

Falk, Richard A. "The Relations of Law to Culture, Power, and Justice." *Ethics* 73 (1961) 12–27.

Feinberg, Joel. *The Moral Limits of the Criminal Law.* 3 vols. New York: Oxford University Press, 1984–87.

Fish, Stanley. "Working on the Chain Gang: Interpretation in Law and Literature." *Critical Inquiry* 9 (1982) 201–16.

Fortas, Abe. *Concerning Dissent and Civil Disobedience.* New York: New American Library, 1968.

Fuller, Lon L. *The Morality of Law.* New Haven: Yale University Press, 1964.

Gerwirth, Alan. "Civil Disobedience, Law, and Morality: An Examination of Justice Fortas' Doctrine." *Monist* 54 (1970) 536–55.

Grey, Thomas, ed. *The Legal Enforcement of Morality.* New York: Alfred A. Knopf, 1983.

Hacker, P. M. S., and Joseph Raz, eds. *Law, Morality, and Society: Essays in Honour of H. L. A. Hart.* Oxford: Clarendon Press, 1977.

Hart, H. L. A. *The Concept of Law.* London: Oxford University Press, 1961.

———. *Punishment and Responsibility: Essays in the Philosophy of Law.* London: Oxford University Press, 1968.

Holmes, Oliver W., Jr. "The Path of the Law." *Harvard Law Review* 10 (1897) 457–78.

Hughes, Graham. *The Conscience of the Courts: Law and Morals in American Life.* Garden City, N.Y.: Doubleday Anchor Books, 1975.

Jackson, John S. III. "Shall We Legislate Morality?" *Review and Expositor* 73 (1976) 173–77.

Jenkins, Iredell. *Social Order and Limits of Law.* Princeton: Princeton University Press, 1980.

Kelsen, Hans. *Essays in Legal and Moral Philosophy.* Edited by Ota Weinberger; translated by Peter Heath. Boston: D. Reidel Publishing Co., 1973.

Leiser, Burton M. *Liberty, Justice, and Morals: Contemporary Value Conflicts.* New York: Macmillan Co., 1979.

Lurkings, E. H. "Bureaucracy and Moral Order." *Expository Times* 87 (1975) 17–21.

Lyons, David. *Ethics and the Rule of Law.* Cambridge: Cambridge University Press, 1984.

McCoy, Thomas R. "Logic vs. Value Judgment in Legal and Ethical Thought." *Vanderbilt Law Review* 23 (1970) 1277–96.

Mahoney, Kathleen E. "Obscenity, Morals, and the Law: A Feminist Critique." *Ottawa Law Review* 17 (1984) 33–71.

Marty, Martin E. "Morality, Ethics, and the New Christian Right: Charisma or Compromise?" *Hastings Center Report* 11 (August 1981) 14–17.

Mill, John Stuart. *On Liberty.* New York: Liberal Arts Press, 1956 (originally published 1859).

Mitchell, Basil. *Law, Morality, and Religion in a Secular Society.* London: Oxford University Press, 1970.

Murphy, Jeffrie G., and Jules L. Coleman. *The Philosophy of Law.* Totowa, N.J.: Rowman & Allanheld, 1984.

Nozick, Robert. *Anarchy, State, and Utopia.* New York: Basic Books, 1974.

Pannenberg, Wolfhart. "Toward a Theology of Law." *Anglican Theological Review* 55 (1973) 395–420.

Parent, W. A. "Privacy, Morality, and the Law." *Philosophy and Public Affairs* 12 (1983) 269–88.

Paulson, Stanley L. "Classical Legal Positivism at Nuremberg." *Philosophy and Public Affairs* 4 (1975) 132–58.

Poythress, Norman. "Behavior Modification, Brainwashing, Religion, and the Law." *Journal of Religion and Health* 17 (1978) 238–43.

Rawls, John. *A Theory of Justice.* Cambridge, Mass.: Harvard University Press, 1971.

Raz, Joseph. *The Authority of Law: Essays on Law and Morality.* Oxford: Clarendon Press, 1979.

Richards, David A. J. *The Moral Criticism of Law.* Encino, Calif.: Dickenson Publishing Co., 1977.

Roberts, T. A. "Law, Morality, and Religion in a Christian Society." *Religious Studies* 20 (1984) 79–98.

Rostow, Eugene V. "The Enforcement of Morals." *Cambridge Law Journal* (1960) 174–98.

St. John-Stevas, Norman. *Life, Death, and the Law: Law and Christian Morals in England and the United States.* Bloomington, Ind.: Indiana University Press, 1961.

Sartorius, Rolf. "Social Policy and Judicial Legislation." *American Philosophical Quarterly* 8 (1971) 151–70.

Smith, M. B. E. "Is There a Prima Facie Obligation to Obey the Law?" *Yale Law Journal* 82 (1973) 950–76.

Stewart, M. A., ed. *Law, Morality, and Rights.* Dordrecht: D. Reidel Publishing Co., 1983.

Stumpf, Samuel E. *Morality and the Law.* Nashville: Vanderbilt University Press, 1965.

Sturm, Douglas. "Crisis in the American Republic: The Legal and Political Significance of Martin Luther King's *Letter from a Birmingham Jail,*" *Journal of Law and Religion* 2 (1984) 309–24.

Terrell, Timothy P. "Flatlaw: An Essay on the Dimensions of Legal Reasoning and the Development of Fundamental Normative Principles." *California Law Review* 72 (1984) 288–342.

Toulmin, Stephen. "Tyranny of Principles." *Hastings Center Report* 11 (December 1981) 31–39.

Wasserstrom, Richard A., ed. *Morality and the Law.* Belmont, Calif.: Wadsworth Publishing Co., 1971.

———. "The Obligation to Obey the Law." *UCLA Law Review* 10 (1963) 780–807.

Wellborn, Charles. "Public Versus Private Morality: Where and How Do We Draw the Line?" *Journal of Church and State* 20 (1978) 491–505.

Wolfe, Robert Paul. *In Defense of Anarchism.* New York: Harper & Row, 1970.